INTERRUPTING HATE

Homophobia in Schools and What Literacy Can Do About It

Mollie V. Blackburn

Foreword by Katherine Schultz

Teachers College, Columbia University
New York and London

Portions of the poem, "For Barbara, who said she couldn't visualize two women together," are reprinted with permission from Ellen Bass. The poem originally appeared in F. Howe (Ed.), *No more masks! An anthology of twentieth century American women poets*. New York: HarperPerennial.

Published by Teachers College Press, 1234 Amsterdam Avenue, New York, NY 10027

Copyright © 2012 by Teachers College, Columbia University

Library of Congress Cataloging-in-Publication Data

Blackburn, Mollie V.,
    Homophobia in schools and what literacy can do about it / Mollie V.
  Blackburn ; Foreword by Katherine Schultz.
      p. cm.
  Includes bibliographical references and index.
  ISBN 978-0-8077-5273-9 (pbk. : alk. paper)
  ISBN 978-0-8077-5274-6 (hardcover : alk. paper)
    1. Homophobia in schools--Prevention. 2. Toleration--Study and teaching. 3.
  Literacy--Study and teaching. I. Title.
  LC212.8.B53 2012
  370.86'64--dc23   2011031850

ISBN 978-0-8077-5273-9 (paper)
ISBN 978-0-8077-5274-6 (hardcover)

Printed on acid-free paper
Manufactured in the United States of America

19 18 17 16 15 14 13 12   8 7 6 5 4 3 2 1

Interrupting Hate: Homophobia in Schools and
What Literacy Can Do About It
MOLLIE V. BLACKBURN

Playing Their Way into Literacies: Reading, Writing, and
Belonging in the Early Childhood Classroom
KAREN E. WOHLWEND

Teaching Literacy for Love and Wisdom:
Being the Book and Being the Change
JEFFREY D. WILHELM & BRUCE NOVAK

Overtested: How High-Stakes Accountability Fails English
Language Learners
JESSICA ZACHER PANDYA

Restructuring Schools for Linguistic Diversity:
Linking Decision Making to Effective Programs,
Second Edition
OFELIA B. MIRAMONTES, ADEL NADEAU, & NANCY L. COMMINS

Words Were All We Had:
Becoming Biliterate Against the Odds
MARÍA DE LA LUZ REYES, ED.

Urban Literacies: Critical Perspectives on Language,
Learning, and Community
VALERIE KINLOCH, ED.

Bedtime Stories and Book Reports:
Connecting Parent Involvement and Family Literacy
CATHERINE COMPTON-LILLY & STUART GREENE, EDS.

Envisioning Knowledge:
Building Literacy in the Academic Disciplines
JUDITH A. LANGER

Envisioning Literature: Literary Understanding and
Literature Instruction, Second Edition
JUDITH A. LANGER

Writing Assessment and the Revolution in Digital Texts
and Technologies
MICHAEL R. NEAL

Artifactual Literacies: Every Object Tells a Story
KATE PAHL & JENNIFER ROWSELL

Educating Emergent Bilinguals: Policies, Programs, and
Practices for English Language Learners
OFELIA GARCÍA & JO ANNE KLEIFGEN

(Re)Imagining Content-Area Literacy Instruction
RONI JO DRAPER, ED.

Change Is Gonna Come:
Transforming Literacy Education
for African American Students
PATRICIA A. EDWARDS, GWENDOLYN THOMPSON MCMILLON, &
JENNIFER D. TURNER

When Commas Meet Kryptonite:
Classroom Lessons from the Comic Book Project
MICHAEL BITZ

Literacy Tools in the Classroom:
Teaching Through Critical Inquiry, Grades 5–12
RICHARD BEACH, GERALD CAMPANO, BRIAN EDMISTON,
& MELISSA BORGMANN

Harlem on Our Minds:
Place, Race, and the Literacies of Urban Youth
VALERIE KINLOCH

Teaching the New Writing: Technology, Change, and
Assessment in the 21st-Century Classroom
ANNE HERRINGTON, KEVIN HODGSON, & CHARLES MORAN, EDS.

Critical Encounters in High School English: Teaching
Literary Theory to Adolescents, Second Edition
DEBORAH APPLEMAN

Children, Language, and Literacy:
Diverse Learners in Diverse Times
CELIA GENISHI & ANNE HAAS DYSON

Children's Language:
Connecting Reading, Writing, and Talk
JUDITH WELLS LINDFORS

The Administration and Supervision of Reading Programs,
Fourth Edition
SHELLEY B. WEPNER & DOROTHY S. STRICKLAND, EDS.

"You Gotta BE the Book": Teaching Engaged and
Reflective Reading with Adolescents, Second Edition
JEFFREY D. WILHELM

No Quick Fix: Rethinking Literacy Programs in America's
Elementary Schools, The RTI Reissue
RICHARD L. ALLINGTON & SEAN A. WALMSLEY, EDS.

Children's Literature and Learning:
Literary Study Across the Curriculum
BARBARA A. LEHMAN

Storytime:
Young Children's Literary Understanding in the Classroom
LARWRENCE R. SIPE

Effective Instruction for Struggling Readers, K–6
BARBARA M. TAYLOR & JAMES E. YSSELDYKE, EDS.

The Effective Literacy Coach: Using Inquiry to Support
Teaching and Learning
ADRIAN RODGERS & EMILY M. RODGERS

Writing in Rhythm:
Spoken Word Poetry in Urban Classrooms
MAISHA T. FISHER

Reading the Media: Media Literacy in High School English
RENEE HOBBS

teachingmedialiteracy.com: A Web-Linked Guide to
Resources and Activities
RICHARD BEACH

What Was It Like? Teaching History and Culture Through
Young Adult Literature
LINDA J. RICE

Once Upon a Fact: Helping Children Write Nonfiction
CAROL BRENNAN JENKINS & ALICE EARLE

Research on Composition
PETER SMAGORINSKY, ED.

Critical Literacy/Critical Teaching
CHERYL DOZIER, PETER JOHNSTON, & REBECCA ROGERS

(Continued)

For volumes in the NCRLL Collection (edited by JoBeth Allen and Donna E. Alvermann) and the Practitioners Bookshelf Series
(edited by Celia Genishi and Donna E. Alvermann), please visit www.tcpress.com.

This book is dedicated to my mom,

Miriam Nicholas Williams Blackburn
(1936–2010),

who taught me how to stand strong when it came to the things that mattered to me, even when doing so went against the things that mattered to her.

Contents

Foreword

When I was in college, my friends and I read a magazine article which asserted that the term "gay" was a "tragic misnomer," given how difficult life was for those who self-identified as gay. There is no doubt that this statement was true at that time—the early 1970s—and, as Mollie Blackburn asserts and illustrates in this wonderful book, it remains true today. Yet at that time my friends and I found it almost laughable. In our college bubble, we were certain we would soon achieve full rights for gays and lesbians, and a future of universal equality and happiness.

But in our narrow struggles and victories, in a very particular world, we failed to realize, and to feel on a daily basis, the constant micro-aggressions experienced by those of us who did not identify as straight. We could add explicit lesbian and gay films to our college human sexuality courses, start a women's studies program, claim *The Dialectic of Sex* as our touchstone text, and, if we were straight, have commitment ceremonies to stand in solidarity with our gay friends who did not have the right to legally marry (little did we know that decades later we'd still be fighting the battle for gay marriage state by state). Yet we still understood the world through gender binaries and did not have the vocabulary to talk about gender identities or wrestle with the complexities of moving outside of proscribed categories. We did not even have the vocabulary—or the analysis—to fully understand the construct of allies, though it was a stance many of us attempted.

Looking back, it is clear that we were too sanguine about our own positions and the work we each needed to do, not only to be comfortable with our own sexualities, our gay and straight friends, and the movement in between, but, for those of us who were straight, to become effective allies in the world beyond our bubble which wasn't quite as benign and accepting. In Blackburn's words, we were not "always becoming an ally"—that is, doing the difficult work necessary to continually listen, pay attention, and keep learning.

In this important and powerful book, Mollie Blackburn provides teachers, students, parents, youth workers, community members, and policymakers—in brief all of us—with poignant stories, current research, and lived understandings to inform how we can act to make this a safer world for all youth, and especially for those who identify as LGBTQQ (Lesbian, Gay, Bisexual, Transgender, Queer, and Questioning). With a focus on literacy, Blackburn illustrates the critical importance of standing up, again and again, for all youth who are marginalized. She gives concrete, tough, honest, and positive suggestions for how we can take principled, moral, and ethical stands against the injustices perpetrated upon the youth and colleagues in our lives who may be bullied, scared, or scarred by the actions and words of others. She suggests means of taking action, and points to the complexities of what might seem simple. It's not always the best policy, for instance, to discuss a gay-themed book in class, if there aren't protections for students who may be identified as LGBTQQ. Inviting youth to compose narratives about their experiences is important, but the invitation must be made in a way that mitigates risks, negotiates threats, allows for a way out, and surrounds the work with love and thoughtfulness.

This emphasis on love and care permeates this book. Blackburn insists that we confront homophobia and heterosexism, yet she propagates this tough-minded insistence with gentle ideas, support, and the suggestion that we take action with love and acceptance. She explains that "the most effective way of being an ally is by always becoming an ally," emphasizing the importance of continually educating oneself to be an ally, and offering a rich discussion of what this means, as well as a set of concrete strategies for how to do it. Whether the reader identifies as gay or straight, queer or transgendered, Blackburn offers new and critical insights that push each of us to act more intentionally and thoughtfully in support of all youth.

This book presents difficult material. It is painful to read the stories of youth denied an equitable education because of their sexual identities. At the same time, these stories are critical to a lived understanding of the issues Blackburn addresses. And the book ends on a hopeful note with concrete steps we can take to make this a more just world. We have no other choice.

—Katherine Schultz, Mills College

Acknowledgments

I am deeply appreciative of the many individuals who helped me shape a life that allowed for the work that resulted in this book. The young people represented here, as well as other youth, gave so generously of their time and insights and continue to share relationships with me into their adulthood. The teachers constantly remind me of the changing realities of schools and what is (im)possible there. Susan Lytle, Kathy Schultz, Celia Genishi, and Meg Lemke never lost confidence in the idea that one day I might have something worth saying about the work I was doing (or if they did, they never let me know, and I am grateful for that). Jolley Christman and Elaine Simon encouraged me to consider LGBTQ youth centers as places to hang out, listen, and learn; and Larry Sipe suggested that I read and discuss *Am I Blue?* with the youth in such a center. I am indebted to each of them for their guidance.

I thank Carrie Jacobs, Kristen Hopkins, Susan Freeman, Angie Wellman, Glenn Zermeño, and Jen Gilbride-Brown for making me feel at home at The Attic and Kaleidoscope. I thank Caroline Clark for making me feel at home in the Midwest and for being such a significant collaborator on the projects we've conducted there, particularly for funding the books we shared in the literature discussion group. I am also grateful for the Research Foundation of the National Council of Teachers of English for funding several years of the teacher inquiry group. Mindi Rhoades and Lauren Kenney did the tedious work of reading early drafts and providing valuable feedback. Valerie Kinloch coached me through the process of writing a book that someone might eventually want to publish. Dinnertime discussions with Kelly Magee helped me struggle with what it means to write and to be a writer.

And then there are the people who bring balance to my life, some of whom I've already mentioned. Conversations over Clintonville meals with the Magee-Kenneys, Noah, the Clarks, and the Crider-Podalsky crew; Philadelphia walks with Patrick, Jon, Kelly, and Deborah; and long car-rides to and from Virginia and Georgia with my partner Mindi and children Blais

Marie and Dottie Grey made not only this book possible but my life possible. Thank you for your love, humanity, and constant striving to be the best versions of yourselves. How fortunate I am to be among you.

Part I

THE PROBLEM

The problem of homophobia, a "socially produced form of discrimination . . . against homosexuals" (Murray, 2009, p. 3), for young people in U.S. schools could hardly be ignored during the fall of 2010. "In September 2010 alone, at least six gay youth—all of whom endured a relentless stream of taunts by their classmates—ended their own lives" (Burford, 2010, ¶2). Whether this report represented an increase in suicides or even suicide attempts by lesbian, gay, bisexual, transgender, queer, or questioning (LGBTQQ) youth is not known; but media attention to gay (male) teen suicides indisputably surged. By focusing on gay youth as victims of homophobia, media recalled constructions of these young people typical in literature from the 1960s and scholarship from the 1970s. In these constructions, gay youth needed to be protected from bullies who needed to be punished.

The protect-and-punish approach, though, is both ineffective and distracting. It is ineffective, in part, because it relies on the fictional notion of "the bully" and the false premise that any one person is monolithically a victim and that another is monolithically a bully. By focusing on bullying, rather than homophobia, the approach points to the problem of bullies as individuals rather than the systemic problem of homophobia, in which all of us are implicated. Even if we could isolate the problem to the bullies, who are the bullies? What if they are also the victims? I have frequently heard LGBTQQ youth talk about classmates who they believed to be gay making homophobic comments. Katrina, for example, a male-to-female trans-youth, confessed,

> I'm not going to lie, I did it too. Before I came out. I used to pick on people who were flamey, I used to pick on them. No fucking lie. It was this boy named Jon. This boy was so fucking flaming I used to

pick on him all the time. [I'd say,] "Oh, he a faggot." . . . He walks
around like, "Oh child. Girl, whatever, yeah. Oh my god, and he is
so," and I used to pick on him just because it was so hard for me to
come out.

Many people in U.S. schools are, in more subtle ways, both victims
and bullies, particularly around norms related to gender and sexuality.
To pretend otherwise fails to capture and, thus, to address adequately the
complexity of homophobia.

The protect-and-punish approach also distracts from the real change
that needs to happen, that is the dismantling of oppressive institutions,
including schooling. Schooling is one of the most damaging institutions
to LGBTQQ youth, specifically. In part, the damage schools do to
LGBTQQ youth is under the guise of protection: patronizing citizens
protecting public school students/recruits/victims from LGBTQQ
adults/predators/bullies. (It is interesting to note how in this dynamic,
LGBTQQ people are the bullies, just as monolithically but inversely.)
Consider, for example, the purging of gay and lesbian teachers from
Florida schools led by Anita Bryant, among others, in 1977 (Blount,
2006; Graves, 2009). At that time, teachers perceived to be gay or lesbian
were fired in an effort to protect the public school students of Florida.
Although I am drawn to the idea of having come a long way since
then, I am disheartened as I recall that the same tactic of positioning
voters as protectors of public school students against LGBTQQ adult
predators was used in California in 2008 by supporters of Proposition
8, the California Marriage Protection Act, which recognized marriage
as only between a man and a woman. Even though this constitutional
amendment was about marriage, supporters of Prop 8 argued that if
the proposition did not pass, then teachers would teach public school
students that gay marriage is okay. This dynamic, past, present, and even
in relationship to issues that would seem to be not particularly related
to school, such as Prop 8, perpetuates the idea that schools that allow
LGBTQQ teachers to work with students or LGBTQ-themed content in
curricula are failing to protect students. Good schools, alternatively, keep
LGBTQQ people and content away from students. It is no wonder, then,
that LGBTQQ kids feel like they don't belong in schools and that many

students work hard to stay away from all things understood to be queer. It is no wonder that schools are typically homophobic institutions.

The damage of homophobia is not confined to, in Murray's words, "homosexuals." More generally, homophobia is directed at anyone who is not heterosexual, such as bisexual people, or heteronormative, such as people who identify as transgender or transsexual. By heteronormative, I mean adhering to social rules and regulations that privilege biological men who behave in stereotypically masculine ways, such as being attracted to women. Heteronormativity also privileges biological women who behave in stereotypically feminine ways, but not to the extent that it privileges men because imbedded in heteronormativity is misogyny. *Heterosexism* is a related word, but it names something more subtle: the often subconscious assumption that everyone is straight or the belief that straight people are inherently better than those who are not. So an example of a homophobic comment is, "I heard the Latin teacher is gay, so I'm taking German." In contrast, an example of a heterosexist comment is asking a girl whether she has a boyfriend. Both contribute to the oppression LGBTQQ youth experience in schools.

Thus far, I have used the acronym LGBTQQ in an attempt to be as inclusive and specific as possible. I use the term queer, the first *Q*, in reference to people who are not heteronormative but prefer to evade more specific classifications such as lesbian, gay, bisexual, or transgender. *Questioning* refers to one who is questioning one's sexual identity. Often, but not always, this is someone who has always assumed his or her heterosexuality and is just beginning to question that assumption. Throughout this book, though, I will use the acronym, term, or word used by the source on which I'm relying. The source may be scholarship or it may be youth at one of two youth centers I discuss, both of which use *LGBTQ* in which the single Q stands for *questioning* (not for *queer*). Alternatively, the source may be an individual, in which case I will use the term s/he uses to name him/herself, such as *dyke*. People identify themselves in thoughtful, deliberate, and strategic ways that I may or may not understand but that I wish, at least, to respect. This is a reasonable approach for teachers and youth service providers to take as well.

The oppression LGBTQQ youth experience in schools and how it impacts academic achievement and literacy learning is the focus of this first section of this book. The section, comprising only one chapter, draws on current scholarship to offer a portrait of homophobia in schools that is both broad and deep. Then I turn to the relationships between the problem of homophobia in schools and academic achievement, ultimately focusing on literacy learning in particular. These relationships are illustrated with people you will come to know throughout the rest of the book, including LGBTQQ and straight-ally youth. By looking outside of schools, in queer friendly contexts, we can learn more about how LGBTQQ youth make space for themselves and others like them in schools and how straight-ally students and teachers can support and contribute to these efforts.

1

The Problem of Homophobia in Schools and What Literacy Has to Do with It

In Gray's (1999) book entitled *In Your Face: Stories from the Lives of Queer Youth*, queer youth reported being in fights, getting spit on, overdosing on drugs, and dropping out. They describe their school experiences as "strictly hell" (p. 81), "miserable" (p. 82), and "abusive" (p. 85). More recently, and even in a community renowned for being queer friendly, David, a Black gay male, said, "People used to think I was a girl and I used to get teased a lot because of that. . . . People eventually started throwing things at me and shit" (McCready, 2004a, pp. 138–139). Kim Murray (1998), like the youth in Gray's and McCready's studies, also pointed to the abuse she encountered in school. She challenged her readers to

> Imagine walking down the hall of the place in which you are expected to learn and not being able to go a day without being called names as: psycho, dyke, dyke bitch, homo, lesbo, and anything else a teenage imagination can come up with when referring to your known, suspected, or rumored sexual orientation. . . . Imagine your classmates going as far as threatening your life if you dared going to your senior prom with the one you cared about. (p. 131)

But she also asked her readers to consider, "How about receiving little or no help from teachers or other adults because they could care less or are simply afraid of being labeled with the same tag as you?" (p. 131).

Teachers often fail to intervene in their schools' homophobia. Youth are vulnerable to such abuse and neglect regardless of whether or not they are "out," or openly gay. Dylan, for example, was an out gay student who was threatened in his school's parking lot when a group of students lassoed him and proposed tying the "faggot to the back of the truck" (Human Rights Watch, 2001, p. 1). When Dylan reported the event, he was told "not to discuss his sexual orientation with other students" (Human Rights Watch, 2001, p. 1). Somkiat, on the other hand, didn't talk to other students about his sexual orientation. Even though he was "closeted" at school, his classmates perceived him to be gay. He described his school experience in this way:

> Everyday they make fun of me and stuff. They call me gay and faggot and stuff. And, when I'm in class, people, guys don't want to sit by me because they think I'm going to touch them and whatever. . . . When I'm late for class, I really don't want to go in because I'm scared [that] when I walk in they'll make fun of me. They always do that. My teacher, she sees it too. She always talks to me after class is up. . . . I feel like there's nobody there to protect me. (Ngo, 2003, p. 118)

THE BIG PICTURE

Homophobia in middle and high schools is ubiquitous, as the Gay, Lesbian and Straight Education Network (GLSEN) document in their biannual National School Climate Survey of lesbian, gay, bisexual, and transgender (LGBT) students in the United States. In the most recent and comprehensive report (Kosciw, Diaz, & Greytak, 2008), 86.2% of LGBT students experienced verbal harassment because of their sexual orientation and 66.5% because of their gender expression (p. xii). This report also shows that 44.1% of LGBT students reported having been physically harassed because of their sexual orientation and 30.4% because of their gender expression. Moreover, 22.1% of this population reported being physically assaulted because of their sexual orientation and 14.2% because of their gender expression (p. xiii).

An earlier version of the GLSEN survey revealed that when even one teacher works against homophobia in a school things are better for the LGBT students in that school (Kosciw, 2004), and even though "eight out of ten students could identify at least one school staff member whom they believed was supportive of LGBT students at their school" (Kosciw et al., 2008, p. 100), LGBT students, like Murray, reported that teachers tended not to engage in anti-homophobia work. According to the 2007 GLSEN survey, "only a tenth (10.5%) of all students in the survey were exposed to positive representations of LGBT people, history, or events in their classes" (p. 99). One might think that even teachers who wouldn't include LGBT topics in their curriculum might still interrupt hateful language related to sexual and gender identities, but "less than a fifth of the students reported that school personnel frequently intervened ('most of the time' or 'always') when homophobic remarks and negative remarks about gender expression were made in their presence (17.6% and 14.6%, respectively)"

(Kosciw et al., 2008, p. 20). According to this report, when LGBT students told school staff about "incidents of victimization, students most commonly said that no action was taken" (p. 41). And, shockingly, this study found that 59.7% of LGBT youth reported hearing homophobic language and 67.7% reported hearing biased language about gender expression from teachers or other school staff (p. 19). Not only are many educators neglecting to make schools more hospitable for LGBTQQ students, some are actively contributing to the hostility these youth experience.

A recent study revealed that adults in schools expel nonheterosexual students at a higher rate than their heterosexual peers relative to their transgressive behaviors (Himmelstein & Brückner, 2010). The study drew on data from the National Longitudinal Study of Adolescent Health (Add Health). Researchers identified nonheterosexual youth by examining responses to questions about same-sex attraction, same-sex romantic relationships, and LGB self-identification and correlated these with school expulsion, among other institutional sanctions. They already knew that nonheterosexual youth were more likely to have engaged in transgressive behaviors, which is not surprising considering the hatred they endure and the fact that they are more likely to have to support themselves outside of their families' homes at a younger age (Ray, 2009). So, in order to learn about increased sanctions imposed on them, as opposed to their heterosexual peers, the researchers controlled for transgressive behavior, among other things. Himmelstein and Brückner (2010) found that "nonheterosexual adolescents, particularly girls, suffer punishments by school and criminal-justice authorities that are disproportionate to their rates of transgressive behavior" (p. 54). As they write, this finding implicates "schools, police, [and] courts but also other youth-serving health and welfare systems that often fail to meet the needs of nonheterosexual adolescents" (p. 55). Adults in schools and youth service providers, nationwide, have a great deal to learn about meeting the needs of nonheterosexual adolescents.

LGBTQQ YOUTH SPEAK OUT

These national studies are humanized (Freire, 1998) by the stories of the people you will meet in this book. In the second section (chapters 2 and 3), for example, you will come to know Justine, an African American lesbian. Justine came out in middle school, first to herself and then her family. She said she was a good student in middle school. Her parents and she selected an arts-based magnet high school in Philadelphia for her, believing it would be a positive place for her as a lesbian. However, when she came to high school, she said, "It was just like constant harassment in the hallways. Just people calling me names, and calling me dyke and all kinds of stuff. I didn't know what to do." As a result, Justine stopped focusing on her schoolwork, started cutting classes, and started staying home because she felt sick. She said,

> I didn't want to move. I didn't want to do anything to draw attention to myself, so I was just like, I would sit there and, I had like a spell check little like thing and it had games on it so I would play games instead of paying attention in my classes.

A teacher noticed her withdrawal and referred her to a guidance counselor who dismissed her claims of harassment, which continued, and, according to Justine, "It got worse and worse and worse and it was like I was rarely ever in school because I was sick." Her mother took her to doctors who identified the problem as stress-induced. Justine told her mother about the homophobia she was experiencing. Her mother talked with the counselor and then the principal. They both dismissed Justine's concerns, until her mother threatened to file suit against the school.

In the fourth chapter of this book, you will meet Anna, Isaac, and Jeff, all of whom go to the same high school in Columbus, Ohio. These students echoed the findings of GLSEN studies: They experienced homophobia in their schools and found that teachers sometimes failed to interrupt homophobic behavior and other times contributed to it. Isaac, a gay, White male, described the homophobia at their school in terms of inequities between straight and gay couples. He said,

> Walking through the hallways there can be a girl and a guy making out right there, teachers can see it, some of them don't say anything, some don't really care. . . . But all you have to do is, if you're gay or you're a lesbian, and you walk with your boyfriend or your girlfriend, just holding hands, you're not doing anything. Then "ooh, Satan has just walked past you," and the entire school is going to go up in flames.

Anna, a Mexican-American, straight ally, reflected on the school's climate for gay people in the same discussion. She said, "[teachers] hear [*gay* and *faggot*] like right in front of them and they don't say a word" and gave a recent example of when she witnessed a teacher failing to intervene in homophobic speech. She went on to describe another incident when a teacher didn't just ignore but, even, exacerbated a student's homophobia by punishing the abused student right along with the abusing one. She talked about how these two students "got into it" in class after John called Jerome a "fucking faggot." The teacher punished both students, even though Jerome had not done anything either to instigate the insult or in response to it. Anna explained that Mr. Peterson's decision to punish both students revealed the teacher's support of John and disapproval of Jerome. It was unavoidable to punish John, who had cursed aloud in class, but almost irrational to punish Jerome, who was sitting at his desk. This accords with the Add Health study showing that nonheterosexual adolescents are punished more relative to their transgressions than their heterosexual peers.

NOT JUST LGBTQQ YOUTH

We see in these stories how homophobia in the school not only affects LGBTQ students or those perceived as such, but also straight allies, like Anna. Anna knew her ally stance could make her vulnerable. When she told the story about Jerome and John, she also said that she wouldn't report the teacher because, in her words, "I don't want to get in trouble." Anna believed that if she had exposed the teacher's behavior, then she would have been penalized.

Homophobia in schools also makes teachers, both LGBTQQ and straight allies, more vulnerable. For example, in Chapter 5, you will meet Lauren and Jill. Lauren, a White lesbian, had administrative support for being out in her arts-based charter high school in Columbus, Ohio, and had positive relationships with her students. Still, the father of one of her students accused her of trying to recruit the student into the "gay lifestyle," and another student was withdrawn from the school because his mother did not approve of the "lifestyle of some of the teachers" (Kenney, 2010). Jill is a White, straight ally who taught high school English and sponsored her school's GSA (Gay-Straight Alliance). Early in her anti-homophobia work in her school, Jill came to recognize the privileges that came with her racial and sexual identities, but this recognition of her privileges came in their dissipation. That is, the more aggressively she asserted herself as an ally, the more she was avoided, dismissed, and silenced. Eventually, her loss of privileges took the shape of her loss of the job, although she was rehired when she threatened to file suit against the district (Smith, 2010).

There is a wide range of people whose space at school is diminished or eliminated by homophobia in schools. When I talk about "space," I mean a living, breathing context characterized by complexities and often conflicts, as exists in any place brought to life by diverse people with unique and evolving personalities. I draw this notion from de Certeau (1984), Talburt (2000), and hooks (1994). Space is defined by de Certeau as a "practiced place" (p. 117). Talburt (2000) expands on de Certeau's distinction between space and place by describing space as "emergent, incomplete, and unpredictable" (p. 19) and place as "an order of distributed relationships, location, and fixity, such as a given culture to be transmitted, an interpretation to be learned, or defined skills and methods of reasoning to be acquired" (p. 19). I understand this to mean that *places* exist in and of themselves, but *spaces* are places brought to life. Even more, space is the people within a place and the ways in which that place brings people to life. In other words, I understand space as a dialogic between place and people. According to hooks (1994), space is

> a context where we can engage in open critical dialogue with one another, where we can debate and discuss without fear of emotional collapse, where we can hear and know one another in the difference and complexities of experience. (p. 110)

Although she is talking specifically about space among women, the notion seems applicable more broadly. When I talk about space, I am talking about the space, or lack thereof, that LGBTQQ youth find or make to explore their identities, particularly their sexual identities, in ways that often conflict with the heteronormative. When I say that a space is "safe enough," I am not characterizing any place as always safe for everyone. What is safe for Jill may not be safe for Lauren, and what is safe for Lauren may not be safe for her student. Further, what may be safe for Lauren at one time may not be at another time.

Space at school is constricted by homophobia for LGBTQQ students and teachers, those who are perceived as such, and even their straight allies. In fact, Lipkin (1995) argues that even homophobes are negatively impacted by homophobia in schools because "hate is a debilitating burden to carry around" that limits one's "understanding of the human experience" (p. 36). Combating this form of hatred in schools is important work to do on behalf of everyone who inhabits them.

IMPACT ON LGBTQQ STUDENTS' ACADEMIC ACHIEVEMENT

The negative impact of homophobic schools on the academic achievement of LGBT students is well documented. For example, Teddy, a Filipina-American, Catholic student, withdrew from school when she came to understand herself as lesbian in her junior year. She reported,

> I loved school. I excelled academically until high school. . . . However, in my third year, my grades dropped dramatically, I stopped going to classes for

weeks at a time, and I just barely graduated. What changed? I realized I was a lesbian in my junior year. I was depressed and withdrew from interacting with my friends from school. Mostly, I would skip class to spend my days in a park alone with a book or my guitar. Although there were a few on-campus resources for queer youth, they were never announced publicly and I never knew of them. (Consolacion, 2001, p. 84)

Teddy is certainly not alone in this sort of experience.

GLSEN found that three-fifths of LGBT youth reported feeling unsafe at school—so unsafe, in fact, that about one-third of LGBT students, like Justine, reported skipping at least one day of school in the month prior to completing the survey (Kosciw et al., 2008). Of course, when youth aren't in school, they don't do as well academically, as the GLSEN report indicates:

> The reported grade point average of students who were more frequently harassed because of their sexual orientation or gender expression was significantly lower than for students who were less often harassed. For example, the grade point average for students who were frequently physically harassed because of their sexual orientation or gender expression was almost half a grade lower than for other students (2.8 versus 2.4). (Kosciw et al., 2008, p. 84)

This inverse relationship between experiences with homophobia and achievement in school has been evident in my work with LGBTQQ youth as well.

Kira, for example, whom you will come to know better in the second section of this book, shifted from an engaged, successful student before she came out to a former student who was pushed out of school. She is a biracial, working-class dyke raised by an African American foster mother, and she attended the same magnet high school for the arts in Philadelphia that Justine attended. She described her school experience after coming out in this way:

> I had friends that just stopped talking to me and never explained why. . . . I didn't really care that I didn't have any more friends. I just wouldn't, I just wouldn't go to school. . . . It's really hard to sit at a lunch table if you don't talk to anybody. . . . When you go to the same school for four years, and then, your senior year, you're alone, you're just like, "OK," so you don't go to lunch, then, eventually, you just don't go to school. (Blackburn, 2003b, p. 43)

The problem of homophobia in schools is detrimental to academic achievement in general and literacy learning in particular. In his study of low-income urban high school students and writers, Goldblatt (1995) found that marginalization impedes students' literacy practices. According to him, marginalized people are those "whose private lives are at odds with the dominant view of a proper public persona" (p. 152). LGBT youth in schools are, indeed, marginalized, as Britzman (1997) observed that "schools mediate the discourses of private and public work to leave intact the view that (homo)sexualities must be hidden" (p. 192). Goldblatt found that "a gap between private and public self creates an inhospitable climate for writing. . . . Writers who are alienated from or insecure within the institutional framework of their writing task will predictably have trouble composing texts for that institution" (Goldblatt, 1995, p. 152). Although Goldblatt's study is not focused on LGBT students, Moje and MuQaribu (2003) and Vetter (2010)'s claims of the significance of sexual identities in literacy learning support this application of Goldblatt's findings.

READING LGBTQ-THEMED TEXTS IN SCHOOL

Some teachers have tried to address the problem of homophobia in schools and the impact of it on literacy learning through their teaching of literature. Carey-Webb (2001), for example, describes the work of Pankop, whose high school students read Coville's (1994) "Am I Blue?" the title story in a collection of young-adult, lesbian and gay-themed stories. Athanases (1996) focuses on Liu, whose high school students read and wrote responses to "Dear Anita: Late Night Thoughts of an Irish Catholic Homosexual." Hoffman (1993) writes about his own work teaching Fierstein's play *Torch Song Trilogy* to his high school students, and Greenbaum (1994) explains her efforts to have her students examine gay and lesbian subtexts in canonical works. Although the majority of examples are in high schools, Hamilton (1998) describes his experience teaching the gay-themed young adult novel *Jack* to his middle school students. Schall and Kauffman (2003) write about Kauffman's efforts to discuss literature with gay and lesbian characters with her elementary school students. And Epstein (2000) documented a unit Stuart did with his 9- and 10-year-old students on families, in which he included texts representing families headed by same-sex couples. Although these examples offer hopeful contrast to the results of the GLSEN study, they are not impeccable.

As Clark and I (2009) note in our review of this scholarship, the classroom work mentioned above tended to *position* readers and texts in ways that could exacerbate, rather than alleviate, homophobia in schools. Positioning, as conceptualized in positioning theory, is a "way of reading and understanding the dynamic of human relationships within a social constructivist paradigm" (Luberda, 2000, p. 2). More specifically, positioning is a "discursive process whereby selves are located in conversations as observably and subjectively coherent participants in jointly produced story lines" (Davies & Harré, 2001, p. 264). It can be interactive, where one person positions another, or reflexive, where a person positions him- or herself. The process is ongoing and often unintentional. For example, a teacher might position students as straight and even homophobic by introducing an LGBTQ-themed text with something like, "The text we'll read next raises issues that might make you uncomfortable or even threatened, but I want you to read it with an open mind, willing to learn about people different than yourselves." This conveys to students that the teacher recognizes them not only, as not LGBTQQ, but also as made uncomfortable by topics related to LGBTQQ people. A student might position him- or herself as homophobic by saying aloud upon perusing an LGBTQ-themed text something like, "What's this text about fags? I'm not reading anything about fags." Such a comment establishes the student as not gay and as having no desire to be associated with anything that is related to gay people.

According to Clark and my (2009) review of students reading LGBTQ-themed texts in classrooms, teachers never positioned students as LGBTQQ or straight allies, nor do students assume such positions for themselves. Instead, students were positioned, by teachers and themselves, as straight and often homophobic, sometimes even vehemently homophobic, as in the example above. Moreover, teachers positioned LGBTQ-themed texts as non-normative by providing only singular engagements with this literature rather than multiple opportunities for students to read texts with such themes. Also, teachers typically positioned texts "in ways that privileged didactic purposes over pleasure or political action" (Clark & Blackburn, 2009, p. 27). That is, they only used LGBTQ-themed texts when they had something more easily defensible to offer, like a unique literary form. The teachers, however, are not to blame. Rather, the realities of homophobic norms permeating most schools are at fault. Still, teachers, like all in schools, are implicated in the perpetuation of such norms.

The students you'll meet in this book highlight how homophobia hinders youth's literacy learning in schools. Justine actively rejected the reading and writing she did for school. I saw her carrying around two books, one of which was assigned for school and the other she selected to read. I watched her read the school book until she was nodding off, put that one down in exchange for the self-selected book, and continue to read. I heard her explain that the black and white composition notebook with stickers of the local center for LGBTQ youth and a Spice Girl that she carried around was "just [her]" and that her school journal had "nothing in it." Justine's lack of engagement in school-based literacy was a portion of what she called a wall that she erected to protect herself from homophobia at school:

> At school, who I was as a person, was threatened, and I was sort of, just being harassed for being gay is sort of like, every time you go back to the same place where, you know, something bad has happened to you, either you go right back into feeling how you did before, or you put up a wall . . . to protect yourself.

Jeff and Anna also experienced homophobia as an obstacle to literacy-based learning in school. They went to high school together, but I came to know them in a literature discussion group at the local center for LGBTQ youth. They were there at our very first meeting in the fall of 2006, when we discussed *Boy Meets Boy* (Levithan, 2003). The cover of this young adult novel, light blue with an image of three candy hearts, in pastel colors, with the title words—*boy, meets, boy*—written on them in hot pink, clearly indicates that it is about same-sex desire. Both Jeff and Anna reported being targeted for reading this book in school. According to Jeff, some boys in his science class said,

> "*Boy Meets Boy*, what's that some queer book?" And I was like, "It's about homosexuality, yes." And then they were like, "Well why are you reading it? Are you gay too?" And I was like, "So what if I am?" And then they said, "Well you better stay away from me," and all that other stuff.

Here, Jeff's sexuality was called into question as a result of reading a book that was obviously about same-sex desire. Anna was also targeted for reading the same book. According to her,

> Like my friend, Craig, he always, he's very, very, very homophobic. And, like even, when I had this book I was reading, when I was done, he said, "Is that *Boy Meets Boy*?" And I was like, "Yeah." And he was like, "Are you reading a gay book?" And I was like, "Yeah, do you have a problem with that?" And he was like, "I don't even want to touch it."

When students, at least when these students, voluntarily read LGBTQ-themed books, they were at-risk for homophobic reactions, whether the reader self-identified as gay or lesbian, even when the text was sanctioned by a teacher, in this case the GSA advisor. It is worth noting that the next book selected by the literature discussion group was *The Perks of Being a Wallflower* (Chbosky, 1999), a book in which the gay character is peripheral and the cover is quite plain with nothing even suggestive of gay content.

The literature discussion group contemplated what it might be like to read LGBTQ-themed books in school in almost all of our book discussions. It was evident that reading these books in school had some appeal. Isaac talked about reading *The Perks of Being a Wallflower* and *Finding H. F.* (Watts, 2001) in his classes instead of doing his assigned class work, and Anna talked about skipping class in order to read *Finding H. F.* Isaac also said, at the end of last year, "Ever since this book club, I've been reading a lot more. I'm always like, 'I need a book. Right now.'" In other words, the books are engaging, more engaging than some class work. While this seems to suggest that these books should be read in school, the group called this into question. Anna said,

> I think that people who are not so close-minded and open would enjoy the book and find that the book's not just about gay people, and find it's more than that. And then, but, I still think that there will be people who would just hate it and hate them.

They also talked about how parents would intervene in such efforts. Later, Anna said whether she would even want to read LGBTQ-themed books in class would depend on the teacher and how able he or she was to control homophobia in her classroom.

They did not seem to believe it would work, and they were sad about it. Anna talked about an experience with a friend of hers who "doesn't like necessarily agree too much" with homosexuality, but "she just read *The Perks* and she's like quoting it like every day. . . . She really likes the characters a lot, now like she's more open and everything." For Anna, this demonstrated how homophobia in schools can limit the broader literacy and learning that can be accomplished in classrooms. As she said, "it's sad because you could learn so many . . . views of everything, and then maybe they could understand more." These young people thought their classmates would learn to be more accepting of different people if they read literature like that we read and discussed in our literature discussion group, but that homophobia in school prevented such opportunities.

IN AND OUT OF SCHOOLS

Homophobia in schools and its impact on academic achievement is a significant reason we are beginning to see the opening of public schools that cater to this population, for example, the Harvey Milk School in New York City and, more recently, a comparable school being proposed in Chicago. The Milwaukee Public School System has even approved, unanimously, the nation's first gay-friendly middle school (Calefati, 2008). I am not alone in worrying about charter schools draining funds from public schools, nor am I alone in worrying about what it means to segregate a marginalized population rather than fighting the hatred that fortifies the need or desire for segregation. Still, I have known and continue to know too many youth who may have been able to maintain their status as students and achieve in school had a school that caters to LGBTQQ youth been available to them. I both want these schools to exist and want them to be unnecessary.

What will it take to change the status quo? Although I deliberately position LGBTQQ youth as victims in this section, in an effort to provoke motivation to work for change, I spend the remainder of the book looking at LGBTQQ youth as agents, at students and teachers as allies, and at all of these people as activists. As educators, we need to see our students and ourselves in a new way in order to create schools where LGBTQQ youth can safely and productively work together with allies, even if among those who are not.

In doing so, I focus primarily on out-of-school contexts—a youth-run center for LGBTQ youth in Philadelphia; an LGBTQ-themed literature discussion group in Columbus, Ohio; and a teacher inquiry group, also in Ohio—collectives committed to combating homophobia in schools. As a former teacher and current educational researcher working mostly with students and teachers, I continually wonder, "so what does this out-of-school work mean for schools?" But, I deliberately rely on conversations and observations in queer friendly, out-of-school contexts. By queer friendly, I mean a space that is generally positive for LGBTQQ people and people who are perceived as such, and their straight allies. Such spaces are imperative for learning about LGBTQQ students as anything other than victims, because the homophobia that is so prevalent in schools often squashes the agency and activism out of LGBTQQ youth.

READING AND WRITING WORDS AND WORLDS

To explore the anti-homophobia work accomplished through literacy, I've pointed to examples of people reading and writing traditional print-based texts. This is the most commonly accepted understanding of literacy. However, in the following chapters I'll expand the notion of literacy to include the reading and writing of texts construed broadly to include electronic texts, visual images, films, and, even more broadly, the world. That is, following the lead of Freire (1987), I consider the reading and writing of words *and* worlds. Freire and Macedo (1987) state,

> Reading the world always precedes reading the word, and reading the word implies continually reading the world. . . . This movement from the word to the world is always present. . . . We can go further and say that reading the word is not preceded merely by reading the world, but by a certain form of *writing* it or *rewriting* it, that is, of transforming it. . . . This dynamic movement is central to the literacy process. (p. 35)

Embracing the vitality and transformative potential of literacy does not require romanticizing literacy into a sort of unmanageable everything. But, we need to acknowledge that reading is only one of many ways of interpreting or consuming, and writing is only one of many ways of composing or producing. And trying to understand reading and writing *words* in isolation from *worlds* is all but useless. With that in mind, I advocate examining reading and writing words, or texts, and worlds, or contexts, in relationship to each other in order to grasp the vitality of literacy.

Freirian notions of literacy embrace literacy as potentially transformative, both in terms of individuals' agency and in terms of society more broadly. With respect to individuals' agency, literacy is a tool that offers its users opportunities to control thoughts and emotions (Vygotsky, 1986) so that we can "position ourselves for ourselves" (Holland, Lachicotte, Skinner, & Cain, 1998, p. 64), or develop and assert our agency. But Giroux (1987) claims that literacy is not only about individuals in society but also about individuals on society. He states that literacy is "inherently a political project in which [people] assert their right and responsibility not only to read, understand, and transform their experiences, but also reconstitute their relationship with the wider society" (p. 7). In other words, literacy can be used as a tool for making one's life more bearable but also for making the world a more socially just place.

PRACTITIONER APPLICATIONS: INTERRUPT HATE

This book is relevant, not only for teachers and youth service providers of LGBTQQ students, but for those of any marginalized youth. Literacy is one way to combat homophobia, but it's also a tool for fighting all sorts of oppression.

For example, this chapter shows concretely the hatred that LGBTQQ youth experience and how it hinders their academic achievement and literacy learning. It challenges teachers and youth service providers, indeed, anyone who is invested in the education of young people, to do something about this hatred:

- Know that the diversity of your students is not always visible.
- Stop people from using slurs; teach them what they mean; explain their consequences.
- Prevent fights by addressing tensions.
- Interrupt violence.
- Do not let fear prevent you from doing what you know is right.
- Recognize your biases.
- Pay attention to your students; talk to them when something seems wrong; be open to hearing about their lives beyond school; if you are unable to address their concerns, connect them with someone who can.
- Familiarize yourself with community resources.
- Recognize allies in the context in which you work; connect with them.

Throughout this book, I will continue to add to this list of suggestions. As we learn from LGBTQQ students and allies and their teachers, I hope you will come to value the work of these agents, advocates, and activists and maybe even come to see yourself among them.

Part II

LGBTQQ YOUTH AS AGENTS AND ACTIVISTS

The second part of this book focuses on LGBTQQ youth as agents and activists, showing first how they use literacy to make space for themselves in queer friendly contexts and then how they make space for themselves in schools. This section draws primarily on my 3 years of work as a volunteer, employee, and researcher at The Attic, a youth-run center for LGBTQ youth ranging in age from 12 to 23.

The Attic offered a wide array of services such as support groups, counseling, tutoring, and social activities. It served a diverse population of youth, at least in terms of race, class, and gender, although almost all of them were from urban communities. I am reluctant to list the demographics of The Attic, in part, because I buy into the Foucaultian (1982) argument that when people can be labeled or named, they can be controlled. He claims that oppressed people need to reject such naming. He states that "taking the forms of resistance against different forms of power [is] a starting point" (p. 780), but that we, in reference to oppressed people, need to "promote new forms of subjectivity through the refusal of this kind of individuality which has been imposed on us" (p. 785) in order to free ourselves from oppression. But I also buy into Harstock's critique of Foucault. She claimed that Foucault wrote "from the perspective of the dominator," in terms of being a white male, and therefore, his postmodern perspective allowed "systematically unequal relations of power to vanish" (p. 165). From her perspective, it was easy for someone with power to dismiss categories of power. She asserts that Foucault's postmodernism is a "dangerous approach for any marginalized group to adopt" (p. 160) because oppressed people need to be able to name power dynamics in order to work against them.

Adding to this philosophical concern is a practical one: It seems like
I just won't get it right, and perhaps I can't. This struck me one evening
as I sat in the lobby of The Attic, among youth, going through the
attendance lists, trying to establish some statistics about the population.
I went through the lists, name by name, turning each name into a tally
that fit in a box of a grid that I had designed to be so efficient. I used
The Attic's racial categories African American, Asian Pacific Islander,
Caucasian, Latino, and biracial or other, and the gender categories male
and female. I did not feel great about the categories, but I forged ahead.
The only modification I made was to complicate gender, that is, I also
included male-to-female transgender and female-to-male transgender.

As I came to the names of people whom I did not meet or did not
remember, I asked the youth around me what boxes I should mark.
Several people became interested in what I was doing. They sat beside
me, asked me questions, tried to help me. I read Christopher Smith
and assumed the person was male. Someone told me that's Katrina.
Oh, of course! So, African American male-to-female? No, she's biracial,
"Haven't you ever seen her sisters?" So, with guidance from the youth,
I marked biracial or other male-to-female; Katrina was someone I
knew fairly well. This kind of dilemma happened over and over again.
Someone reminded me that Jessica Moore was Steve. Another person on
the list told me that he was not African American but multiracial, and he
listed the many races with which he identified. The tallying task seemed
daunting and worthless. I put it down. I still haven't finished it.

Hence my reluctance to share the demographics of The Attic. But,
I want to offer some description of who was there. According to The
Attic's statistics, the youth served were 45% African American, 40%
European American, 5% Latino/a, 4% Asian Pacific Islander, and the
other 6% are either of other ethnicities or of mixed ethnicities. In terms of
gender, the statistics say that 54% of the youth were male and 46% were
female. In my experience, The Attic was most heavily used by African
American males. The school district in which The Attic is located and
where many of the youth went to school was 63.8% African American,
19.8% Caucasian, 11.6% Latino American and other, and 4.7% other
ethnicities. Eighty-two percent of these students were eligible for free

or reduced-price lunch (Rhoades & Wittenberg, 2001). It is also worth noting that this district had a policy that is defined as a

> process designed to foster knowledge about and respect for those of all races, ethnic groups, social classes, genders, religions, disabilities, and sexual orientations. Its purpose is to ensure equity and justice for all members of the school community, and society as a whole, and to give those members the skills and knowledge they need to understand and overcome individual biases and institutional barriers to full equality. (Board of Education, School District of Philadelphia, 1994)

These statistics and this policy were just that: statistics and policy. They were not the lived experiences of the youth of The Attic.

There is a song called *Home* written by Tom Wilson Weinberg, a long-time adult supporter of The Attic. Dara, as a youth and later as an adult staff member, used to sing it at Attic events. Some of the lyrics are

> Home is where I am, not my childhood home, not my parents' home.
> Home is where I am, where my time is spent, where I pay the rent, where I hang my hat, mow the lawn, set the thermostat, watch the dawn . . .
> Home is where you are, not your childhood town, not your parents' town.
> Home is where you are, where your books are kept, where you overslept, where your slides are shown, keys are lost, plants are grown, clothes are tossed . . .
> Home is where we are, not some distant spot, not the family plot.
> Home is where we are, where we spend our nights, where we fights our fights, where our friends can stay, where we telephone, set a breakfast tray, be alone.
> Home.

In my mind, The Attic was a home, a home filled with tensions, challenges, and love.

This home serves as the center of the next two chapters. Chapter 2 focuses on how LGBTQ youth use literacy to make space for themselves in queer friendly contexts such as The Attic. In doing so, it shows youth developing agency. Chapter 3 is a look at how LGBTQ youth use literacy to make space for themselves in schools, which are typically hostile contexts for this population. Thus, this chapter represents youth asserting their agency. Together, these chapters of the second section build an argument for LGBTQQ youth as agents and activists.

2

Developing Agency
in Queer Friendly Contexts

Just walking up the four cement steps to the glass door of The Attic, one could tell it was a queer friendly space. The door was almost always covered with fliers and posters, with signs and symbols like rainbows and inverted pink triangles, which could only be interpreted by people who had at least some knowledge of LGBTQQ communities. Others could walk down the two-lane, one-way street and never even notice the red brick row-house. This discretion was deliberate, so that LGBTQQ people might read or recognize the place as queer friendly but homophobes may not. Teachers and youth service providers have much to learn from places like The Attic precisely because they are queer friendly, but also because of the sophisticated literacy performances engaged in by youth in these contexts, as this chapter will show.

LITERACY PERFORMANCES

The concept of literacy performances is grounded in New Literacy Studies and builds on Street's (1999) definitions of literacy events and practices. According to Street (1999), "literacy events" are "observable behaviors around literacy" and "literacy practices" focus on "cultural practices with which uses of reading and/or writing are associated in given contexts" (p. 38). Hornberger (2000) further distinguishes literacy practices by noting that practices are "both observable patterns of behavior across events . . . and the more ideological aspects which are not directly observable" (p. 344). She goes on to describe "the more ideological aspects" as "underlying norms, values, and conventions" (p. 344).

This sociocultural understanding of literacy practices is compatible with Freirian notions of literacy as well. In Freirian terms,

> Reading does not consist merely of decoding the written word or language; rather, it is . . . intertwined with knowledge of the world. Language and reality

are dynamically interconnected. The understanding attained by critical reading of a text implies perceiving the relationship between text and context.
(Freire & Macedo, 1987, p. 29)

As discussed in Chapter 1, these emancipatory understandings of literacy
emphasize the importance of agency and activism.

That LGBTQQ youth develop agency, or strengthen their capacity to
act in and on the world, through literacy practices in queer friendly contexts has been documented qualitatively in several other contexts. De Castell and Jenson (2007) documented queer and questioning street-involved
youth in Canada as they participated in the Pride House project, the prima-
ry purpose of which was to raise funds for housing for this population. The
youth were hired and trained to design and implement an ethnographic
study of the population of which they were a part. The young researchers
conducted individual and group interviews, focus groups, and observations; took photographs; collected survey data; analyzed documents; re-
viewed research literature; engaged in art-based activities; and produced
video and audio recordings and a finished video. The research team used
multimodal documentation and composition because the youth found it
more compelling and because it foregrounded their expertise. Through this
work, the youth researchers developed agency by using literacy to describe
themselves, their situations, and their needs on their own terms.

Halverson (2007) also studied queer youth using literacy in a queer
friendly context to develop agency. She studied a Chicago-based program
called About Face Youth Theatre. In this program, LGBTQ adolescents
told their own stories about being queer youth, sometimes orally, other
times in writing. The group listened to or read the stories and adapted
them into scripted scenes that they ultimately performed in a Chicago the-
ater. Thus, LGBTQ youth used literacy to develop agency as they worked
to represent themselves through a dramaturgical process.

Driver (2007) explored queer girls and popular culture, particularly
queer girls' engagement with alphabetic texts such as lesbian magazines
and online communities as well as television, film, and music. Her study
revealed how these girls found "inventive ways . . . [to] deploy media in
their everyday lives, deriving pleasures while challenging and questioning hegemonic ideologies" (p. 242). They developed agency as queer girls
by simultaneously enjoying and critiquing texts that represented them
and people who are in some way like them.

By bringing Judith Butler's (1991, 1999) performance theory, which
depends on queer theory and feminism, to New Literacy Studies, one can
conceptualize literacy in terms of performance. According to Butler, one

performs one's identities over and over and over again. She theorizes that this repetition serves not only to solidify but also to destabilize identities because in each performance there are slight variations among the previous, current, and prospective performances. Although her theory is about identities, it can inform the notion of literacy. It can highlight relationships among various literacy practices as they take shape in and over time—past, present, and future. If we think of literacy as a series of performances in which we read and write words and worlds, again, here, drawing on Freire and Macedo (1987), then any one performance is among innumerable other performances, each of which is both similar to and different from all of the others, both confirming and disrupting one another. Integral to literacy performances is the agency of readers and writers and the potential for transformation—something not highlighted in either literacy events or practices.

Throughout the queer friendly context of The Attic, youth, quite noticeably, used reading and writing to locate themselves relative to schools, even in this out-of-school context. Many of the youth were legally required to go to school and many more were socially expected to be students. That is, even when youth were old enough to make the legal choice not to attend school, people often assumed that they were in school, or, if they were not, this was assumed to be a failure of some sort. Identities existed in relationship to school, even when youth had dropped or been kicked out of schools, were trying to earn their GEDs (Graduate Equivalency Diploma), or were trying to declare independent status so they could get funding to go to college. Youth engaged in literacy performances that established The Attic as decidedly not school, that actively rejected school, that allowed the youth to imagine school differently, and that mimicked academic literacy. In this way, these LGBTQ youth practiced asserting themselves as LGBTQ people, in increasingly schoolish ways, and thus developed their agency.

NOT SCHOOL

Walking into The Attic, you enter a foyer, with a gray-and-white linoleum floor, cracked in places, and then the lobby, where the opportunities to read and write were seemingly limitless. Many of the texts in the lobby and the ways in which they were used communicated that The Attic was decidedly not school. They conveyed that in this place, LGBTQ youth were not alone, they had the right to learn about themselves, and they did not have to be victims.

Not Alone

Because youth learn early on that being anything other than straight and gender normative is something to conceal, youth who question their sexuality and/or gender identities generally do not see other people embodying what they are feeling. As a result, they can feel as if they are all alone. You might hear young people talk about how they are the only ones in their families, schools, and communities who feel the way they do in terms of same-sex attraction or who experience their gender less dichotomously.

In the lobby of The Attic, there were whiteboards and fliers on the doors and the walls that advertised social support groups at The Attic, such as Story Time and Women's Group. These texts were ubiquitous, and they conveyed that there were other LGBTQ youth who wanted to meet, talk, and socialize. There were also fliers that advertised upcoming community events, such as vogueing contests, the alternative prom, and the gay-pride parade. There were stacks of newspapers, such as the *Philadelphia Gay News* and *au courant*, local papers by and for local LGBTQ communities. Cards from donors were also tacked up on the walls. At various times throughout any given year, youth would come together in the lobby and create, sign, and address cards for supporters of The Attic. These cards, both to and from donors, reminded youth of adults outside of the center who valued the center and the youth who came there in very concrete ways.

Reading the room, youth learned there were groups structured for LGBTQ youth support and socializing, there were communities of LGBTQ people in their immediate area, and there were adults who supported LGBTQ youth. In short, they were not alone.

Not Victims

Sometimes when youth who are questioning their sexual and/or gender identities look around, they see one or two people who are "like them," but are victims of homophobia and/or heterosexism. For example, a young man experiencing same-sex attraction may look at his flamboyant male classmate who is understood by others to be gay, whether he identifies as such or not, and see him being teased, taunted, and abused. The first young man may not feel alone, but he likely feels terribly vulnerable. The social rule of concealing any non-normative sexual or gender identities is underscored. Added to it is the implication that those who break the rule will be punished.

The reading of the texts in the lobby of The Attic, however, calls that rule and its consequences into question. There was a bulletin board advertising accomplishments of youth who came to The Attic. This offered images of LGBTQ youth who were agents, who were working for themselves and other LGBTQ youth by working against heterosexism and homophobia. Texts in the lobby invited other youth to participate in such work via advertised leadership opportunities, such as serving on the youth planning committee (YPC; a voluntary group open to all Attic youth who were interested in planning events for other LGBTQ youth) and applying for positions on the Speakers' Bureau (a group of youth hired and trained to educate youth and youth service providers about LGBTQ youth).

The texts in the lobby of The Attic communicated that LGBTQ youth could be agents instead of victims by highlighting their accomplishments, inviting them to assume leadership opportunities, and providing them opportunities to work against heterosexism and homophobia.

The Right to Learn About Themselves

In order to assert their agency, though, LGBTQ youth need to learn about themselves. Doing so in schools is challenging, when not impossible, since opportunities to learn about LGBTQ people are constrained by curricula defined by standardized tests and teachers' homophobia and heterosexism. Even when those things are not obstacles, teachers who might otherwise initiate lessons about LGBTQ populations are often fearful of parental and administrative homophobia. Students who might choose topics pertinent to LGBTQ people, for assignments that allow for it, are often fearful of their classmates' homophobia.

There was a bookshelf in the lobby of The Attic that held brochures and pamphlets about various support groups and organizations, such as those about and by Parents and Friends of Lesbians and Gays (PFLAG) and about important, but often taboo, issues such as drug and alcohol abuse and sexually transmitted infections (STIs). The PFLAG brochures and pamphlets provided youth with opportunities to explore what it meant to be lesbian or gay in their families and friendships. The information about drug and alcohol abuse and STIs may not seem to be directly related to LGBTQ youth, but they were important to youth, in general, and these youth in particular. Since, as compared to other adolescents, self-reporting LGBTQ youth are two times more likely to use alcohol, three times more likely to use marijuana, and eight times more likely to use cocaine/crack and are particularly susceptible to contracting STIs due to the denial of their sexual identities (Garofalo, Wolf, Kessel, Palfrey, & DuRant, 1998). These texts helped make The Attic a safer place, where LGBTQ youth could effectively reject, imagine, and mimic school.

REJECTING SCHOOL

Considering how intensely LGBTQQ youth are rejected from schools by administrators who fail to support them via policy, teachers who fail to include them in their curricula, and classmates who ostracize and even abuse them, it is understandable that LGBTQ youth, in turn, reject schools. They do so to protect and assert themselves.

Such rejection was apparent in the literacy performances of The Attic's Women's Group. This group, like most at The Attic, was open and, so, attendance varied. Over the 2 years that I worked with the group, it ranged in size from just one or two young women to as many as twelve or thirteen, but usually there were around four or five attending. There was a core group of young women, mostly African American, who came regularly. Weekly, these young lesbians and bisexual women used literacy to develop their agency by exploring together what it meant to be women-who-love-women.

Television and Film

The group sought and shared representations of women-who-love-women via music, television, film, and written texts. They watched and discussed movies, such as *The Color Purple* (Guber & Speilberg, 1985) and *High Art* (Hall, Levy, & Cholodenko, 1999) and made-for-television movies, such as *If These Walls Could Talk 2* (DeGeneres, Anderson, & Coolidge, 2000), *The Truth about Jane* (Rose, 2000), and *What Makes a Family* (Streisand & Greenwald, 2000). These young women even volunteered for the local gay and lesbian film festival in order to earn free tickets, for example, to a collection of shorts called *Young Dykes in Love*. Through television and film, they explored what it means to different people of various ages across time periods and circumstances to be women-who-love-women but not women who reflect stereotypes of lesbians and bisexual women. The television shows and films they watched and discussed do not portray women-who-love-women as deviant, sick, or sinners. Rather, they are represented as strong women oppressed by heterosexism and homophobia. The young women in this group developed agency by both actively connecting and disconnecting with these texts.

Take, for example, the efforts of these young women to explore the role of sex in sexual identity. Such an exploration is complicated for young lesbians because, so often in our society, when people think of homosexuality, they immediately think of sex, rather than richer, fuller relationships, feelings, and desires. In this way, lesbians are understood as hypersexual, but then there is a conflicting understanding of lesbians, who, as women, are often thought to be asexual or at least much less sexually driven than men. Lesbians are caught in this paradox of societal expectations—as homosexuals they are thought to be sexual, but as women, they are thought not to be. This is a stereotype that young women in the group critiqued, and they drew on texts to bolster their critique.

Watching *If These Walls Could Talk 2* (DeGeneres et al., 2000) helped to disrupt the notion that lesbian relationships, as homosexual relationships, are only about sex and thus led to a deeper understanding of such relationships with respect to love, commitment, and family. For example, the first of the three shorts this show comprises portrays an elderly White woman who was widowed when her life partner, who was also a White woman, died from a stroke. The widow lost much of what she had because their relationship was not legitimized by a legal marriage. Women in the group cried and expressed disgust. Clearly, the group connected with this short film that represented lesbian relationships as being about love, commitment, and family.

The young women, however, also wanted to debunk the idea that women were asexual. Justine, for example, walked with me to select a lesbian safer-sex video for the group to watch. There was a section in the video rental store entitled "Of interest to lesbians," and we perused the collection. We settled on a video called *She's Well*. When I began to show the video to the women in the group, Dara told me it was not the one she wanted, and we did not watch it. About a month later, Justine told me about reading in school, but not for school, *Doc and Fluff* (Califia, 1996), a book with same-sex, sexually explicit scenes. Around the same time, the young women proposed a field trip to a local store that sold erotic clothes, toys, and so on. We made the trip several weeks later and then watched a lesbian safer-sex video that Dara brought to the group.

The significance of their sexual identities, though, expanded beyond love, commitment, family, and sex. It also included, among other identities, their race. Many of the texts that we shared focused on White lesbians and bisexual women. Thus, the young women both connected to and were disconnected from the very same texts. For example, by the end of our viewing of the third short in *If These Walls Could Talk 2* (DeGeneres et al., 2000), several women in the group expressed frustration by the lack of people of color in the show. The group talked about how the collection of shorts seemed to reify the myth that homosexuality is a White issue. The young women in the group were almost entirely women of color; in contrast, almost all of the women in the television and film they watched were White. Kira explicitly talked about the limited representations of African Americans on television, particularly television that includes LGBTQQ people. This same problem existed among the books that youth shared in the Women's Group. For example, a young woman in the group said that she was looking for a book about lesbians that had some sex in it but was not entirely about sex, and Justine suggested that she read Rita Mae Brown's (1988) *In Her Day*. The young woman carried around that book, while Justine carried around one of Brown's (2000) more recent novels, *Loose Lips*, opening and reading them every now and then. Like the videos, these books portray lesbian relationships as sexual, and as much more than that, but they do not offer a lot in terms of racial diversity. The young women actively compensated for this shortcoming within the group by bringing in texts representing people of color. For example, Justine brought in a video of Margaret Cho, a bisexual Korean-American comedienne, and another young woman suggested that we read "'Whose Pussy Is This?' A Feminist Comment" by bell hooks (1996), an African American–ally, and watched *She's Gotta Have It*, Spike Lee's (1986/2008) first feature-length film that, while decidedly heterosexual in focus, acknowledges African American women as in charge of their sexuality. In these and other ways, the group discussed issues surrounding race and sexuality almost every time they met and even produced its own text in order to represent themselves in all of their diversity.

Self-Representation

The first such text was a flier to distribute at the local gay-and-lesbian film festival. They talked about how these fliers would advertise our group and invite others to join us. They selected a name and photograph and wrote a description of the group; each of these pieces drew from and contributed to the group's understanding of what it meant to be women-who-love-women.

For starters, in coming up with a name, some people suggested Sappho's Garden and Isle of Lesbos, drawing from a traditional idea of what it means to be lesbian—the former referring to the Greek poet who wrote love poetry to women and the latter referring to the island where that poet was born. Others suggested Circles in a World of Rainbows to reference women in male-dominated gay communities, in which circles represent women and rainbows represent some gay communities. The only suggestion that served to name differences among women-who-love-women was Teas & Granola to Whips & Chains. This name seemed to dichotomize women who some people call "crunchy" and those who are sadomasochists—and invite in women all along this continuum. Aunt Flow, a euphemism for menstrual cycle, was suggested in jest, but it drew some fairly clear lines excluding transgender women.

Initially, the young women in the group neither accepted nor rejected any of these suggestions; they continued to play with words and possible names. And, playfully, they came up with Snack Time on the Magic Carpet, which they explicitly identified as a double entendre—literally referring to food being central to our group and figuratively referring to cunnilingus. It was a clear derivative of the term *carpet munchers*, a derogatory term for lesbians. The youth, despite adult resistance, assertively claimed the name.

The young women in the group developed their agency by writing words to name themselves, as a group. By accepting a name that not only reclaimed but also played with a hateful term, they simultaneously rejected the hypersexualization of homophobes and embraced their own sexuality. Moreover, they used the name in strategic ways among other LGBTQ youth. They said it to one another in a jocular manner, playing with the sexual innuendo and their own sexuality. They explained the meaning of the name to other people in The Attic, where there were many more young men than women, thus debunking the notion that women were not sexual. They also said it seriously with no explanation, as a way of putting distance between themselves and the people with whom they were speaking. Also, outside of The Attic, where many people did not seem to understand the name, it served, much like a private joke among friends, to establish a sense of insider-ness or a sense of intimacy among the women in the group. They developed their agency by writing themselves into the world as powerful people with a supportive community.

After selecting a name for the group, they selected a photograph for the flier. One young woman offered several from a stack of photographs in the office of youth at Attic events. These were rejected, though, because they failed to represent the diversity of the group, and so, special group photographs were taken. They finally settled on one showing a group of young women, who were diverse, particularly, in terms of race and ethnicity, body type and physical ability. The women in the photo were also diverse in terms of accessories, attire, and style; that is to say, they were not all butch or femme—some had long hair, some had short hair, some wore gender-neutral clothes, others wore skirts.

By creating, selecting, and ultimately distributing this photograph to represent the group, group members developed their agency by rejecting the notion that being gay is a White thing. They also worked to portray themselves as diverse in ways beyond race by including coupled and single people, short and tall people, thin and fat people, able-bodied people and people with physical disabilities, and butch and femme people. Thus, the photograph disrupted almost any monolithic assumption one could make about women-who-love-women. This was something the group noticed and valued.

A description of the group was also drafted. It named Snack Time on the Magic Carpet as "a support/social group for women—between the ages of 12 and 23—who love women." It included contact and meeting information. The draft was brought to the group to workshop. Describing the group as a "support/social group" ensured that people would not misunderstand the young women as victims needing only support. The group expressed some concern, however, about sounding too old, and implicitly boring, because of the word *women*. There was also some concern about sounding too young, and implicitly naïve, because of the age range starting at 12. Undergirding this discussion was a tension related to the ignorant and offensive connection some people make between homosexuality and pedophilia. Therefore they decided to use *women* but to narrow the age range from 12 to 23 to 16 to 23.

Snack Time on the Magic Carpet was the least school-like among the groups at The Attic, with texts and topics not likely to be school-sanctioned or explicitly valued, and youth-driven pedagogy differing from what one might see in schools. The young women in this group used literacy to develop and activate their agency. In doing so, they rejected school by reading and writing words and worlds that are often prohibited or used hatefully in schools. Story Time, which I discuss next, was also decidedly not school-like. Yet, it was a place where youth imagined what it might be like to use literacy to discuss LGBTQ-themed topics in schools.

IMAGINING SCHOOL

Even though LGBTQ youth have every reason to reject schools, and do, they also have every reason to imagine themselves as a part of school. To imagine a student identity that embraces their LGBTQ identities, they engage in activities that are like those at school in many ways except that they are inclusive of LGBTQ themes. For example, they read, write, discuss, and analyze alphabetic texts that represent LGBTQQ people. Sometimes they even engage specifically with texts from school in the safer space of The Attic, as a way of analyzing these texts with people who are more receptive to discussions of LGBTQ themes. Thus, LGBTQ youth use literacy to develop their agency by engaging in literacy performances that are simultaneously schoolish (Smith & Wilhelm, 2002) and embracing of their lives.

Story Time at The Attic met for 2 hours per week; sometimes the group was small, just a couple of youth, and other times it was as large as eighteen young people. Typically the group included approximately nine youth who came together to read, tell, and listen to stories written by and about LGBTQ people, oftentimes themselves.

Schoolish Texts

Typically, meetings began with youth sharing any texts they had brought, and they brought texts to almost half of the meetings (47%). Of the texts they shared, about two-thirds (67%) were written by the youth and one-third (33%), by someone outside The Attic. Of the 83 unique texts the youth shared, 67 were alphabetic, including poems, journal entries, excerpts from books, letters, short stories, and even an excerpt from the Bible. Non-alphabetic texts included recordings of songs, audiotapes of conversations, videotapes, a piece of art, a photograph, and a scrapbook.

When they did not bring texts, they selected among those that I, as the facilitator, brought and described. Of the texts that I brought, most (80%) were published by someone outside The Attic; the other texts were data, drafts of papers, poems, and journal entries by either my life partner, Mindi Rhoades, or me. I shared 43 unique texts, of which 33 were alphabetic (77%): poems, short stories, articles in periodicals, excerpts from novels, vignettes, written data, a book of questions, and a 'zine (a magazine written, produced, and distributed by an individual for his or her peers, construed broadly). Other texts I shared included audiotapes, videotapes, picture books, and an excerpt from a graphic novel. As diverse as these texts were, the vast majority were, in many ways, like those one would find at school.

Sometimes, although rarely (7% of the time), the youth opted only to tell stories from their lives. More typically, we combined reading some of what they had brought, some of what I had brought, and telling stories about ourselves. As youth told stories about their lives, they regularly revealed school as a place where LGBTQ people were prohibited or ignored as possibilities in the texts they were assigned, or even allowed, to read and write. Once, they brought in a text produced at school about LGBTQ issues, and critiqued it, as I describe below.

A School-Produced Text

On this occasion, Story Time included five Black young women, five Black young men, one White young man, and me, an older (in this context) White woman. We read an article from Headley High School, a local urban public school. The article mentions an anti-homophobia workshop conducted at the high school by an employee of the school district and two youth from The Attic, including one of the young women who was in this particular meeting of Story Time. The article is entitled "I'm Gay! AND?" and illustrated with a pencil drawing of two young women kissing. It begins by stating that it is a response to a question posed to the newspaper staff about why there were so many "dykes" in one of the small learning communities of the school.[1] The author, Barbara, states that the question was close to being a stupid one and wondered why "people think that homosexuals are weird, abnormal, demonic creatures." She explains that "homosexuals" have "dreams and goals" and are "ambitious." Then she asks, "Anyway, who is to say that homosexuality is wrong? And even if it is, who are we to judge those who are homosexual?" She cites different students' opinions on the issue: One communicated adamant disapproval, another expressed distant apathy, and a third stated that homophobia is a result of fear and hate. Next Barbara talks about a question that "caused a lot of controversy" in the workshop at Headley High: "Should or shouldn't a person tell everyone about his/her homosexuality?" She reports that 30% of the people said no and 70% said yes. According to Barbara, those who said no, felt that "it isn't anybody's business unless these individuals start serious relationships," and those who said yes wanted to be saved the "time and humiliation" of going up and talking to someone "homosexual." Barbara points out that "homosexual" students sometimes get teased out of school and suggests that "we need to try to accept them. After all, they are human; we can't deny that."

In reading this text, the youth were expected to imagine school, at least this school, as a place where women-who-love-women certainly exist. By some they are called "dykes" and considered to be "weird, abnormal, demonic creatures." By others they are disregarded, and still others consider them to be humans with "dreams and goals." There are even a couple of people in this school who associate the problem of women-who-love-women with the homophobes rather than the "homosexuals." In such a school, the positionality of lesbian and bisexual women is quite variable. What is consistent, though, is that the women-who-love-women are represented in this article as *them* and not *us*, which made for a rather awkward reading in Story Time. That "we" are straight and "they" are "homosexual" is highlighted in the final note of the article, which reads: "Please note: [Barbara] is not gay. The headline was written to attract the reader's attention and express the main point of the article."

Text Analysis

Through the Story Time meeting, youth analyzed the newspaper article from an LGBT-informed perspective. But first, people in the group began to laugh and talk among themselves. A young woman joked that she had had sex with Barbara; a young man sneered, "Yeah, you're not gay, um hmm, right." They questioned Barbara's maturity and suggested she was homophobic because she identified as straight so unequivocally.

While just writing the article for the school newspaper may have been a risky move for Barbara, intending to support gay students at her school, the LGBTQ youth in the context of Story Time mocked her efforts. Only one young woman acknowledged Barbara as one of the "straight people out there [who are] helping us."

The tone of the article demonstrated that it is a risk to be interpreted, even falsely, as gay at Headley High School. For this author, such risk required her overt rejection of the very identities of the people that she was trying to support. So even though this school, understood through the reading of this article, is a place where women-who-love-women exist, it is also a place where authoring one's self (the term used in Holland et al. [1998]) as lesbian is risky, perhaps too risky for Barbara. As an explicitly named straight young woman, she could argue for the rights of lesbian and gay people, but whether this could be accomplished by youth who identify as something-other-than-straight is unknown.

Self-Reflection

After some discussion about whether people who identify as straight can work for the rights of LGBT people, the group took up the question mentioned in the article: "Should or shouldn't a person tell everyone about his/her sexuality?" In other words, should they, as LGBTQ people, author themselves as such. Perhaps not surprisingly, the only White man in the group responded first. He said, "I don't feel there's no point to come out. If you [women] come up to me and ask me or try to talk to me, like 'oh, you're hot,' or whatever, 'yo, can I have your number?' [I'll say] 'I'll give you my number, but I'm gay.' You know, that's how I feel about coming out." For him, he did not need to identify himself as gay unless he were being romantically or sexually pursued. The next person who addressed the question was one of the young Black men, who said, "The whole coming out thing is not important because it just isn't. That goes into my own person thing, my own personal thing is that I don't use labels." To him, naming himself based on identity markers was in conflict with his values. The third person to respond was Dara, and she said,

> I think it's important for me to be out. Like, not that I would go somewhere and be just be like, "I'm a lesbian" . . . but in situations like when I was in school, that was really important for me to be out and in school now sort of, like, I don't really have many relationships with people in school, but there are certain situations that happen in class that I'm just like, "look, you cannot say this," to my professors and if that brings me out of the closet then fine, I'll have to deal with it, and at work it's important and I want to be able to say that I went out with my partner or something like that, it's important to me.

According to her, it was not only important for her to present herself as a lesbian in potentially romantic circumstances, but also in school.

The tensions in this discussion echo Harstock's (1990) critique of Foucault (1982), discussed in the description of Part II, that is, Foucault argues that oppressed people need to evade labeling because labeling enables oppression and Harstock counter-argues that we must be able to name ourselves relative to inequitable power dynamics in order to defend ourselves. The difference is in who does the naming or, again, to use Holland, Lachicotte, Skinner, and Cain's (1998) terminology, who does the authoring. For example, Dara felt it was important to construct herself as a lesbian in school, but she did not say that she wished to be named by others. Further, when Barbara represented gay people in general while distinguishing herself as "not gay," the LGBTQ people in this group reading her article were offended by her efforts, as evidenced by their mockery of her. This seems key to the discrepancy between Foucault, who asserts there is power in naming and that that power is used to oppress people, and Harstock, who claims that power can also be claimed via language. By claiming the name lesbian, Dara claimed some sense of stability, from which to assert her agency and work against heterosexism and homophobia in her school. In short, by claiming a name, she claimed power.

Barbara, however, did not have to claim a name to claim power. The name she would have claimed, straight or heterosexual, is typically assumed and as such has power, particularly in this school context, which she describes as homophobic. This suggests the importance not only of who does the naming but where the naming is done. In this homophobic context, it was not enough to be assumed to be straight, since this assumption would have been called into question by her effort at advocating on behalf of gay people, but it was also, apparently, not enough to name herself as straight. Instead, she went further, to reject a name that would strip her of power in the context of her school. By marking herself as "not gay," Barbara constructed herself as not "weird, abnormal, demonic," and "wrong," all words she used in her article. Admittedly, she tried to refute these characterizations of gay people, but she did a much better job at characterizing herself as not these things in two short words: *not gay.*

Queer Friendly Context

The youth's close reading of the article did not occur in Dara's or Barbara's school—or any school, for that matter. Instead, this reading occurred in a youth-run center for LGBTQ youth. The Attic was a place where being a woman-who-loves-women was not so terribly stigmatized that identifying as such brought condemnation. Here, there was not only space for authoring themselves into the world as lesbian and bisexual women, but even space for mocking those who actively rejected such authoring. As a result, these youth developed agency by constructing themselves as deserving of human rights rather than relying on others, like Barbara, to do this for them.

This is not to suggest that either The Attic or Story Time was devoid of inequitable power dynamics. It was not (Blackburn, 2003a). In many ways it replicated typical inequitable power dynamics as evidenced by young men speaking before young women and White men speaking before Black men, even when responding to a reading of a text by a woman and, most likely, given the particular school where the article was published, a woman of color. Inequitable power dynamics were also apparent in the fact that I, as an older White academic, facilitated the reading and discussion, instead of a youth of color taking the lead. That youth developed agency through the reading and discussion of texts even among inequities suggests that students can do this work within and against institutions that oppress them, including schools.

In Story Time, LGBTQ youth imagined what it would be like to read and discuss LGBTQ-themed texts in school. They did this by selecting and reading LGBTQ-themed alphabetic texts, which are not typically school sanctioned, in school-like ways, facilitated by a former teacher. Further, they analyzed a school-produced text about gay people in a queer friendly context and practiced challenging heterosexism and homophobia and reflecting on themselves as sexual minorities. Thus, the youth began to see the possibilities of using literacy to help them find and make space for themselves, as LGBTQ youth, in schools. They imagined themselves as agents *against* heterosexism and homophobia, agents *for* social change.

MIMICKING SCHOOL

There are some LGBTQ youth who are particularly motivated to make schools positive places for themselves as well as other LGBTQ people, by working within and against traditional educational systems. In order to accomplish this, they must know, or learn, how to do school well. One way to do so is to mimic school, which the youth did in the Speakers' Bureau.

The Speakers' Bureau was a group of Attic youth who were hired and trained to conduct educative outreaches about LGBTQ youth to youth and youth service providers, including students, teachers, and administrators. During the time that Dara and I worked together in the Speakers' Bureau, we had whole-group planning meetings once per week, small-group planning meetings when necessary, and outreaches when scheduled. The members of the group varied, but there were usually five or six youth on the bureau at any given time. They were selected in different ways over time, but while I was there, the group selected new members by soliciting applications, interviewing strong candidates, discussing their prospects, and making recommendations to a staff member who handled the logistics of employment. When we had new-hires, we scheduled two additional meetings, one for preparing for outreaches and the other for community building and developing comfort with public speaking. Looking closely at some of the planning meetings shows how these young people used literacy in this queer friendly context to develop their agency by mimicking school.

Naming and Defining

Dara had suggested that we needed a glossary to use on outreaches, and I agreed to draft one with her. We started by listing the words in the acronym LGBT as well as *transsexual, transvestite, drag queen, homosexual,* and *heterosexual.* Then Dara added *men who sleep with men.*

In defining these words, we began with lesbian. We discussed whether to refer to ourselves as women, women and girls, or females. We agreed that females did not sound right and to use women instead of women and girls, not because we thought that girls could not be lesbians but because we did not trust our audiences not to make the offensive correlation between homosexuality and pedophilia. Even though we knew many people who recognized their attractions to people of the same gender very early in life, when they were, in fact, girls, and even though the document was to be presented and distributed by LGBTQ youth, we elected not to use any word that suggested youth. Therefore, we defined lesbian as a "term to describe a woman who is emotionally and/or physically attracted to women." By focusing on emotional and physical attraction, we evaded talking about sex. "Emotional attraction" points to the fact that sexual identities are about more than just sex, and while "physical attraction" suggests that sexual identities are in part about sex, it does not explicitly state that. Thus, we worked against the stereotype that LGBTQ identities are solely about sex. We modified our definition of lesbian to define gay, bisexual, homosexual, and heterosexual.

Establishing Parameters

Dara and I used literacy to determine which sexual and gender labels get named—or not—and how those that were named were defined. For example, we discussed whether to include *heterosexual.* Dara pointed out that while most people knew what it meant, some people didn't, and we agreed to keep it on the list. By including heterosexual among other sexual identities, we disrupted normative categorization in which straight people are considered to be normal while other sexual identities are not and, thus, in need of naming and defining. In contrast, we failed to include the word *intersex,* for example. This failure represents our ignorance; it was not until later that we began our training regarding people living with intersex conditions.[2]

We defined *transgender* as "an umbrella term to describe people who identify with the gender opposite his/her biological gender." We considered whether to use *biological* or *assigned* gender. Dara discussed how biological is less accurate but simpler. We considered our audiences again, and revealing our distrust of them, decided to opt for simplicity. Next, we struggled to define *transsexual*. A few days later, I asked a young transsexual woman to help us, and after some deliberation she offered this: "a term used to describe people who take hormones to change their outer appearance to match the gender with which they identify."

Dara defined transvestites as "people who wear clothes typically associated with the gender opposite them for sexual pleasure" and *drag queens* as "men who wear women's clothing for performance purposes." We then added *drag kings* to our list.

When I asked Dara, who is African American, about "men who sleep with men," she explained that some men of color consider "gay men" to mean implicitly "gay White men," and in order to distinguish themselves, these men of color call themselves "men who sleep with men." Then she said the term should not go on the list, after all. She chose to conceal racial divisions and offered a false image of unity among LGBTQ people to audiences that are not only assumed to be mostly straight but also heterosexist and homophobic. She did not trust these readers to respect divisions within LGBTQ communities.

Later, Dara and I shared our draft of a glossary with the Speakers' Bureau as a whole, and the following summer we revised it as a group. Given the composition of the bureau at this time, this move provided an opportunity for lesbians and gay men to respond to the ways in which they had been defined, but it did not allow for other people represented by the glossary to do so. The Speakers' Bureau tried, though, to address concerns of people other than ourselves. For example, we changed the definition of transgender to "an umbrella term used to describe people who identify with the gender different from his/her biologically assigned gender," changing the word *opposite* to *different*, thus discrediting the notion of two opposing genders, and *biological* to *biologically* assigned, in an imperfect effort to complicate the origin of gender.

Dara initiated the glossary project while she was transitioning from youth-staff to adult-staff status at the center. We worked collaboratively to generate and define a list of words, and we solicited help from youth. In this way, the pedagogy was more school-like, that is, initiated by adults who invited youth into their work. The text itself couldn't be more school-like: it was an alphabetic text listing and defining terms intended to educate people on a particular topic that may be unfamiliar to them. In terms of content, this document was decidedly not schoolish. However, within this conventional format, LGBTQ youth worked with LGBTQ adults to define themselves and other members of queer communities on their own terms, albeit in limited ways, with the purpose of educating predominantly straight and even heterosexist and homophobic people in mind.

SCHOOLISHNESS OF LITERACY PERFORMANCES

Even in queer friendly, out-of-school contexts, LGBTQ youth engage in literacy performances with an awareness of how they do or do not relate to schools. Sometimes the youth underscore that these contexts are not schools, even actively rejecting schools; other times these youth imagine what schools could be like, if they too were queer-friendly. In this imagining, youth sometimes even mimic schools in out-of-school contexts. Teachers committed to combating homophobia can make schools better places for LGBTQ youth by reflecting on queer friendly spaces, such as The Attic. This is not to suggest that schools should become like out-of-school youth programs any more than out-of-school youth programs should become like schools (Eidman-Aadahl, 2002). Both offer distinct opportunities for young people and can learn from each other without becoming each other. Looking at the texts and pedagogy of the literacy performances in The Attic provides some guidance for teachers who wish to foster the development of agency of their LGBTQ students.

Texts

Youth at The Attic read both traditional alphabetic texts and other media. The content of the texts taken up was quite different from that typically taught in schools. Almost all of the texts were, in one way or another, about being LGBTQ, a topic rarely included in school curricula (Blackburn & Buckley, 2005; Kosciw et al., 2008).

Teachers can value a wide range of media, and many already do. This range should include school-produced texts and schoolish texts, including those produced and/or consumed outside of schools, as well as movies and television shows. This might consist of popular culture texts (Driver, 2007), but also some less popular texts that foreground topics pertinent to LGBTQQ youth. The texts that teachers select can serve to communicate to all of their students that there are and have been positive and powerful people in the world who experience same-sex attraction and/or gender variance, such as Langston Hughes, Gertrude Stein, Alice Walker, and Oscar Wilde, among many others. Moreover, teachers can invite students to write about their lives for audiences both private and public. Doing so conveys to LGBTQQ students that they are not alone and that they have a right to learn about themselves as LGBTQQ people.

Pedagogy

The schoolishness of the literacy performances in The Attic was apparent in the balance of collaboration between adults and youth. In the least school-like literacy performances, youth created the texts and/or initiated the reading or writing of them. In the most schoolish literacy performances, adults assumed these responsibilities. Most often, though infrastructure was established by adult staff members and youth decided whether to engage with it, and if so, how. Then, adults adapted the infrastructure to foster youth engagement.

In this way, youth engagement played a significant role in pedagogical design. Literacy performances, even when choreographed by adults in the center, happened (or didn't) because the youth chose to participate (or not). Unlike school where attendance is compulsory until the age of 16, and lack of participation comes with penalties that typically result in lower grades, there were many opportunities but few requirements to engage in literacy performances at The Attic. Speakers' Bureau was most like school in terms of being compulsory because the hours youth participated were documented, and they were paid based on their participation.

It is imperative for teachers to reflect on the pedagogy of such literacy performances when they invite their LGBTQQ students to write in both private and public ways. This provides opportunities for LGBTQQ youth to reflect on and represent their experiences as non-heteronormative people in typically heteronormative and often homophobic contexts. Doing so allows youth to name and define themselves on their own terms; it permits them to establish their own parameters. These are all important things to practice as youth develop agency. Such practicing can be informed by the texts discussed, which can be profoundly enhanced if teachers are able to create a safe enough context for young people to analyze these texts from LGBTQQ perspectives. Teachers must be cautious and aware, though, of their responsibilities to keep private writings and readings private and respond in thoughtful, respectful, and helpful ways and, with respect to public writing and reading, to prepare students and themselves for potentially negative consequences. In other words, teachers must be sure they can maintain classroom communities in which LGBTQQ youth are not victims.

PRACTITIONER APPLICATIONS: FOSTER STUDENT AGENCY

Just because youth develop agency, though, through literacy performance, does not mean they assert it in ways that are valued by teachers and youth service providers. For example, LGBTQQ youth may assert their agency by fighting homophobes in school or dropping out of school (Blackburn,

2004). With respect to literacy performances, youth may choose to engage only with television and films that they choose and that focus on LGBTQQ people, for example. Such literacy performances are quite different from those typically valued in schools.

Even so, teachers and youth service providers can foster student agency, not only for LGBTQQ youth, but all marginalized youth by doing the following:

- Accept a broad range of texts in order to include and draw on students' strengths.
- Acknowledge that different contents are appropriate in different contexts and that this benefits youth because it gives them access to diverse perspectives.
- Value and integrate a wide range of media in an effort to provide students with more ways into their schoolwork and more ways of applying what they've learned beyond school.
- Include authors and other people that represent diverse populations (be explicit about who is being represented so that young people can see they are not alone).
- Invite, but do not require, students to draw from their life experiences as they learn.
- Respond to students in genuine, thoughtful, and careful ways when they draw from their life experiences.
- Engage youth in pedagogical decisions.

Again, these suggestions come directly from work with LGBTQQ youth in out-of-school contexts, but they can inform work with diverse populations both in and outside of schools.

This chapter has shown that youth can engage in literacy performances in queer friendly contexts in ways that result in their developing agency as LGBTQQ people. They can read and write a wide range of texts about themselves and people who are, in some ways, like them. In this way, they can make space for themselves. Doing so provides youth with opportunities to practice, in a safer environment, naming and describing themselves as LGBTQQ youth. This practice serves as a foundation for asserting themselves in riskier environments, such as schools, as discussed in the next chapter.

3

Preparing for and Asserting Agency in Schools

The literacy performances that LGBTQ youth engaged in at The Attic prepared them to create space for themselves beyond the center, in general, and in their schools, in particular. This is not, however, to suggest a false dichotomy in which LGBTQ youth read and wrote limitlessly about their sexual and gender identities in The Attic and not at all in their classrooms. This was not the case. One time in Snack Time on the Magic Carpet, for example, a young woman brought the readings she had done in a mini-course on lesbian literature that she took at her urban, private high school. The readings included an excerpt from Winterson's (1985) *Oranges Aren't the Only Fruit*, an excerpt from Anzaldúa's (1987) *Borderlands*, Pratt's (1984) "Identity: Skin Blood Heart" and Rich's (1980) "Compulsory Heterosexuality and Lesbian Existence," among others. Considering what we know about homophobia in schools, this mini-course offering is remarkable.

Yet, no one made a move to read these texts at Snack Time on the Magic Carpet, so the young woman agreed to leave them in my box in the lobby so that they could be borrowed from and returned to the box. Perhaps people borrowed and returned the texts, but we never discussed them in the group or elsewhere. It seemed that to take up these academic texts in Snack Time on the Magic Carpet, as opposed to a lesbian literature course at school, would work to co-construct the group in ways that are reminiscent of school, which for many LGBTQ youth, is unsafe. As a group that defined itself as a social *support* group, to sacrifice such safety would be too risky for some of the young women.

So, just as schools are not monolithically negative spaces for *LGBTQQ* students, The Attic was not a monolithically positive space for LGBTQ *students*. This division between youth centers and schools is not desired by either youth service providers or teachers (Eidman-Aadahl, 2002), but it is sometimes necessary for young people. This does not, however, mean that there is no productive space between the two. Rather, it is the spaces in between, where literacy performances allowed, even facilitated, the crossing of boundaries that separated schools and The Attic, that are the focus of this chapter.

INDIVIDUAL ACTION

An Embracing Space

Youth service providers help youth prepare for asserting their agency in schools simply by providing an embracing space. Sometimes this is enough for a young person with a conflicted relationship with schools. Kira, whom you met in Chapter 1, began to come out as lesbian after she started coming to The Attic. The community not only offered a space for her coming out, it also helped her to assert her lesbian identity, through writing and reading, at her magnet high school for the arts. Kira said about her schoolwork, "I had decided that any report that I had done would be on somebody gay or something . . . because everything else wasn't [gay] . . . it was an opportunity to have something gay in school." The curriculum was lacking in terms of representing LGBTQQ people, and the climate was hostile. Kira talked about how lonely school was after she came out because people were "just being jerks," and, as a result, she ended up eating at a lunch table alone. She also talked about "wanting not to be at school because of all the like stuff [homophobic abuse] that [her friend Justine] was getting." In other words, the threat and impact of homophobia were enough to make Kira feel isolated and like she didn't want to be at school.

But when she first came out, she tried to make space for herself in school, such that her lesbian identity was a part of her schoolwork rather than concealed by it. For example, when she was assigned to create a document that included text and a photograph, she selected a poem she wrote entitled "Of me" and a photograph of herself. In the poem, she describes herself as "Adventuring with Sappho and her woman warriors," thus defining herself as a woman who loves other women. She also wrote about "Building bulldozers, to break through barriers" and "Finding room to laugh when there's no space around." These lines convey her desire for and efforts at making space for herself where no such space seemed to exist. She also did a book report on Melissa Etheridge, an out lesbian musician. Thus, through her school-sanctioned literacy performances, Kira worked hard to "break through barriers" to make space for herself as a lesbian in school. It seems to me that Kira was able to accomplish such "breaking through barriers" because she had an embracing space in The Attic.

But, as school was becoming increasingly intolerable to Kira, she would come to class, collect her work, and leave. Off campus she would do as much schoolwork as she could, return to school, turn it in, collect more assignments, and leave again. One of the assignments she collected from school and brought to The Attic was to write a myth that explained something. Her myth, that she came to entitle "The Existence of Steven," plays off of the Biblically-based homophobic comment that it is wrong to be gay because God started the world with Adam and Eve, not Adam and Steve. Her myth debunks this notion, and asserts that God created, first Adam and Steve and then created "a superior gender, with child bearing abilities." Although, according to her myth, Adam and Eve procreated, Eve was bored and asked God to "make her an equal." God agreed, but insisted that, "only one in ten of her descendants could frolic with members of the same sex." Here, Kira built on her familiarity with research done by Kinsey (1948, 1953) in which he found that one in ten people were homosexual. Then, in her myth, Kira built on her knowledge of Sappho as an ancient woman who loved women by writing that God created "Sappho," of whom Adam was so jealous that he "decided it was wrong to frolic with the same sex." In this way, her myth explains homosexuality, as created by God, and homophobia, as symptom of jealousy. Clearly she drew on her own knowledge of people who experience same-sex desire, but she also drew on her peers at The Attic. In an interview, she described how "people . . . helped me write it . . . [by] throwing out words, like 'frolic,' they were throwing out words for me to use." In the context of The Attic, it was appropriate and engaging to write a text that not only foregrounded gay and lesbian people, which Kira very much wanted to do for her school assignments, but also laughed in the metaphorical face of homophobic beliefs grounded in religion. As such, The Attic provided Kira with what she needed to engage in literacy performances in ways that facilitated her in asserting her lesbian identity in school. (For more on Kira, see Blackburn, 2003b & 2005.)

Providing Resources

In addition to providing an embracing space, The Attic also provided students' resources. Justine, for example, whom you met in Chapter 1 and heard about briefly in Chapter 2, identified a poem she encountered in Story Time that resonated with her and that she used in literacy performances asserting her agency and lesbian identity at school.

It was the summer between her sophomore and junior years of high school, the same school Kira attended, but by this time Kira had graduated. At Story Time, each of us had shared poems; Justine shared a poem that she had written, and I shared Bass's (1993) "For Barbara, who said she couldn't visualize two women together."

Just after the meeting, we exchanged copies. Over a month later, in late September, I saw "For Barbara" neatly folded and tucked into Justine's composition notebook, where she wrote much of her own poetry.

Justine told me she was using it with black-and-white images from Faderman's (1991) *Odd Girls and Twilight Lovers* for a television class that she took in her high school. I suggested that she complement the black-and-white images with brightly colored images from the poem, such as a picture of a California poppy, blueberries, and wild mint—a recommendation that she dismissed. In early November, Justine completed the video and presented it in her class at school. I asked her how it was received, and she offhandedly told me that her classmates giggled a little bit but her teacher gave her an A.

Then Justine brought the video to share at Story Time. It began with her reading the poem. Her voice sounded a little shaky, and she laughed what I understood to be a nervous laugh as she read the poem:

Picture lilacs.
Picture armfuls of lilacs, wet
with rain. Nuzzle your whole face
into the bouquet. Feel the cool drops
on your lips. Inhale.

Picture the ocean
from a cliff.
Stand at the edge, see
how the foam tumbles in
and disperses, watch this heavy water
undulate until you're dizzy.
Lie down.

With one fingertip
touch the flat petal
of a California poppy. Lightly
travel the entire surface.
Close your eyes.

Imagine sun on your eyelids.
Recall the smell of wild mint
and the taste of wild blueberries
and the grace of coming upon a doe
at dusk by a river
and she does not bolt.
She lifts her gaze to you
Before she goes on drinking.

Imagine damp seeds sending out blind roots
     into the generous soil.
Picture the root hairs absorbing the mineral-rich drink.
Feel the turgid green push up
     With a force that splits rock.
Hear the laughter.

   *   *   *

Barbara, open your eyes.
Look at these women. You can visualize
any two
together.

On the video, the initial image of Justine reading the poem was replaced by a series of pictures of groups of lesbians from the Faderman
book—women dressed in stereotypically feminine ways, women dressed
in stereotypically masculine ways, White women, and Black women.
These pictures insured that the viewers would not understand the poem
to be only about poppies, blueberries, and mint, but *about* lesbians. Further, Justine pushed the viewers of her video to understand lesbians as diverse in terms of gender expression as well as race, because, even though
the poem virtually ignores race, the pictures that Justine selected were
of interracial couples and groups, including the closing picture of Justine
holding her then-girlfriend—dark skin encircling light—at the gay-pride
parade. The picture remained on the video the longest and demanded
that the viewers understood that the project was not about some abstract
"other," rather, it was about someone they knew, someone with whom
they went to school. Finally, there was a dedication to my partner and
me, which played on the title of the poem, "For Barbara, who said she
couldn't visualize two women together." The dedication read "For Mollie
and Mindi, who could visualize." The conclusion of the video revealed
that not only was Justine a lesbian, but that she was a lesbian who was a
part of a larger lesbian community that loved and supported her.

By reading and getting a copy of the poem at Story Time, taking it to
school with her to make and share the video, and then bringing the video
back to The Attic to share at Story Time, Justine powerfully engaged in
literacy performances that broke down what Justine called a "wall" that
separated the person she was in and out of school. This allowed her to
assert her lesbian identity and challenge her classmates and teacher to
confront their own assumptions about lesbians, whether those assumptions were that there were no lesbians, at least not at their school, or that

all lesbians looked a certain way. It also allowed her to assert her student identity at The Attic. (For more on Justine, see Blackburn, 2002/2003.)

Teachers may not value adults sharing with young people poetry that might be interpreted as erotica. They might think it is inappropriate, if not perverted, and they might feel threatened by the bringing of such poetry into school. But reflecting on Justine's experience shows how the significance of this poem, at least to Justine, was not at all limited to the erotic. Rather, the ways she illuminated this poem in images foregrounded the importance of Justine's intersecting and marginalized identities. Thus, she made it not only appropriate but also laudable (and tolerable) to share with her teacher and classmates.

Intensive Preparation

Many students require more intensive preparation for bringing out-of-school literacies into traditional classrooms. Take James, for example. James was an African American gay man who went to a public high school that served almost entirely African American students in working- and middle-class communities.

James talked about the homophobia he experienced there, such as walking down the hall with another young man and being shoved by a classmate saying, "Look at this fucking faggot coming down the street. You better watch that," as if James were going to initiate some unwanted sexual interaction with him. He also told me about one male teacher at his high school who "figured since all the young girls liked him that [James] liked him too . . . so he always tucked his butt behind the wall when he saw [James] coming." These reactions to James as a gay man reflect the ludicrous assumption that just because James is attracted to men, he is of course attracted to these particular men. Further, their reactions reflect the homophobic belief that men who are attracted to men will sexually assault other men.

It is important to note, though, that James also found support at his school. In 9th grade, when he came out to his friends, most of whom were girls, many said they already knew and all of them "reacted in such a positive way." And one of his teachers came up to him after a "girl had said something to [him] about being a faggot and all this other stuff" and said to him, "'Don't worry what people say about you.' She said, 'Be you,' and that's it." This kind of support inside of school worked in conjunction with what The Attic provided outside of school.

It was the summer between his sophomore and junior years that James began coming to The Attic, first irregularly and then, within a year, more regularly. That's when we started working together, with Kira and

Justine, on the Speakers' Bureau. As with all of the bureau members, we worked together over time to prepare him to conduct outreach to youth and youth service providers. A part of this training focused on the district's "multiracial-multicultural-gender education" policy, quoted in the introduction of this section of the book. This policy was not fully and consistently implemented, but it gave people who knew about it something to point to when needed. For example, a classmate of James' used a homophobic epithet and the teacher failed to intervene. After class, James went to her and told her about the school district's policy. He then solicited and received support from the teacher who told him to "Be you." By coming to know the policy through his Speakers' Bureau work at The Attic and soliciting the support of an ally with authority at his school, James could challenge the homophobia he experienced in his school and provoke his teacher to do the same.

This effort laid the groundwork for a similar, but larger scale, effort that James attempted in his required senior project. He was working on this project while he was training for the Speakers' Bureau, and he asked Justine and me to collaborate. His goal was to design an outreach for teachers to help them work more productively with their sexual-minority students. Together, the three of us collected, read, and organized resources focused on LGBTQ-inclusive notions of multicultural education throughout November and December of James' senior year. Drawing on our collective resources, we shaped a draft of an outline for such an outreach; we edited and revised the outline over time. Eventually, James had a complete outline that he shared with his teachers. James knew that teachers needed to learn how to meet the needs of LGBTQ students, but through his work on the Speakers' Bureau, he had come to know that he could be the one to teach them.

Ultimately, though, James did not conduct the outreach. Although James could, with support, take an activist stance and work against heterosexism and homophobia in his school, there were limits to what he dared to accomplish. The supports and the oppression he experienced did not negate each other but instead complicated each other. In his school, he was essentially working alone. Although he had friends and a teacher who supported him, they were not fighting the same fight that he was. And to fight this fight alone was risky.

This account challenges teachers in two important ways. Most obviously, the intensive work conducted in youth centers can accomplish so much more if it is actively endorsed in schools. Just consider, for example, what it might have meant to the students yet to come out in James' school if he had managed to implement the in-service he designed. And if this were impossible, a single teacher could have organized an event before or after school to which teachers were invited but not obligated to attend James' in-service.

The other challenge is related to the significance of policy, as suggested by James pointing to his school district's "multiracial-multicultural-gender education" policy when he confronted his teacher about the homophobic epithet going unchallenged in their classroom. This same policy was what Justine's mother pointed to when she threatened to file suit against the school for failing to protect her daughter from homophobia (as described in Chapter 1). These accounts suggest that teachers and youth service providers can work together in designing and implementing policies that advocate for young people. (See Chapter 5 for a discussion of teachers engaging in such efforts.)

Risks

What happened when some of the other youth followed through on turning in LGBTQ-themed work to their teachers? Justine, for example, reports on a time in 9th grade when she had an opportunity to write about a topic of her own choice. She said,

> We finally got an assignment to write about whatever we wanted, so I wrote about—or I think it was [to write about] an important issue, and I wrote about legalizing same-sex marriages. And I put everything I had into this paper. This was the only thing I cared about for about a week and a half. And I just wrote and wrote and wrote and wrote and researched and did everything I had to because I wanted this paper just to be the best.

Here, Justine took a risk. She could have written about anything, but she chose to write about a topic pertinent to her, even though it was a highly contestable one, and, as she reported,

> I handed it in. I got it back. I had an N/A, which is, I don't know what that means in teacher-terms, but uh, it means I have no grade, so I didn't fail and I didn't get anything good.

She went on to explain that the teacher accused her of plagiarizing, and after that

> I just had issues with her. She just did not like me. I remember one day she told me that I was single-minded because I wrote one other paper about, uh, about uh, I was working on a committee for the Dyke March, which is a march for lesbians, and I wrote about, you

know, sort of the fellowship, which was really what I was writing about, and she's telling me I'm one, you know, single-minded, because I wrote about lesbians and I wrote about same-sex marriage, but I wrote about fifty other papers over the course of the school year. Um, that just wasn't, it didn't feel good to me to be in this class, and I just hated writing for her after that. It was just, I'd write my papers on the train, throw em at her. She'd give me a B, I'd be like "huh, you didn't even notice that, you know, I'm not putting any effort."

It cannot be determined, by Justine's account, whether the teacher identified Justine's paper as non-applicable because she thought that it was plagiarized, which Justine fervently denied, or whether she did so because she did not feel that Justine should be writing about topics such as same-sex marriages and dyke marches in school, which Justine suggested was the case. However, what can be drawn from this story is that once Justine *felt* like she could not write about LGBTQ people in this class, her engagement plummeted. In other words, the risks inherent in Justine engaging in LGBTQ-themed work for school were not just that her grades were weaker, she didn't like the class and the teacher didn't seem to like her, but also that she became less engaged in the class and her learning about writing suffered as a result.

As I mention above, this happened when Justine was in 9th grade, but she produced the video on Bass's "For Barbara" in 11th grade, and there were other LGBTQ-themed assignments she did over her years in high school. She did this work within and against the oppressions she experienced in and out of schools at the expense of having a more friendly high school career. This was particularly evident to me on the last day of her junior year of school, when I saw her in the lobby writing in her composition notebook. I asked her whether she was getting back to her own writing. She just shrugged. I asked her whether it was for fun, and she shook her head no. I asked whether she was upset, and she nodded; I asked her whether she wanted to talk, and she handed me her notebook and pointed to two pages.

Through the journal entry, Justine reflected on her 3 years at the high school. She described them as hateful—she was hated at the school and that she hated her experiences at the school. She wrote,

First I gave the building the finger. I took one last look at the hardened gray exterior and walked away. I didn't look back and smile. I didn't look back at all. But in my mind I looked back on the past three years. There wasn't a moment that passed by that I didn't wish I was somewhere else. There wasn't a moment I could let my guard down. There wasn't a moment I felt like I belonged. I hated every moment because I knew hate was waiting for me inside that building. . . . I felt entitled to hate them. . . . I hated everyone and everything with such severity I couldn't think of anything else.

She hypothesized that perhaps she hated people at her school because she was jealous of them, writing, "Maybe I hate the Thems so much because I wish I could live so easily . . . being the perfect teenager," but she did not pursue this hypothesis. Rather, she wrote about the purposes and consequences for the hatred. For one thing, the hatred, or here she wrote "dislike," distanced her from other people and, thus, other people's hatred or dislike. As long as they disliked her, she could keep herself from them. For example, she wrote, "I didn't mind being disliked. I really didn't want to be liked. [To be liked] would mean I'd have to tell the truth." This statement resonated with something she had told me in an interview a couple of months earlier: "At school, I'm a certain kind of person with a certain kind of, I guess, personality, which isn't exactly true to who I really am." The hatred kept her far away enough from her classmates to allow her to maintain a façade, which, in this journal entry, she described as "glass walls." She wrote,

> I thought I was protecting myself. By boxing myself in with glass walls, I'd never been so lonely. Through the glass I could see them, they seemed so close if only I could extend myself to them. That just didn't seem feasible. The thought frightened me. Letting them into my life seemed like everything I wanted, Friends, compassion, understanding, and inclusion.

Being an out lesbian at her school demanded, at least from her perspective, that she isolate and insulate herself. As a result, Justine became lonely, devoid of "friends, compassion, understanding, and inclusion."

These are the risks, as articulated by a student, of what was considered to be the most queer friendly school in the city. Many students with whom I worked attended much-less-queer-friendly schools and simply could not endure them as out LGBTQ youth—at least not as individuals in their schools. As a collective, though, they could.

COLLECTIVE ACTION

The Speakers' Bureau was the only collective at The Attic that went into schools. Its purpose was to educate youth and youth service providers about how to meet the needs of LGBTQ youth. In Chapter 2, I showed how they prepared for going into schools, in part, by mimicking reading and writing more typically associated with schools. They prepared in other ways, such as by educating themselves on the content, rehearsing the different components of outreach, practicing telling their stories in various ways for various audiences, and deliberating over ways to respond to typical questions and critiques. Although the kinds of outreach varied according to the youth conducting them and the specific audiences, among many other things, almost all of the outreach included a discussion of terms, telling stories, and answering questions. Usually we were invited to speak by a teacher or district leader, and the audiences typically comprised teachers and/or students. Speakers' Bureau members, as a collective, analyzed language, talked about the significance of writing themselves in both words and worlds, and instigated important reflections on interactions with LGBTQ people in schools. They strove to make a space for LGBTQ youth in schools and to assert their agency in making this possible.

Analyzing Language

Speakers' Bureau members worked with their school-based audiences to identify homophobia through an analysis of language. In doing so, they not only educated their audience members but also took some degree of control over the language used, at least in the outreach. Typically, a Speakers' Bureau member invited audience members to call out terms used to describe a woman who is sexually and emotionally attracted to other women. In addition to "lesbian" and "homosexual," we often heard, "dyke," "carpet muncher," and "bulldagger," among others. Next the youth invited the audience to call out terms used to describe a man who is sexually and emotionally attracted to other men, and in response we heard "faggot," "butt pirate," and "sissy." For men and women who are attracted to both men and women, audience members called out "switch hitter" and "confused." All during this brainstorming session, a Speakers' Bureau member was writing down the words we heard.

It was important to have audience members voice the words they were likely already thinking of when the outreach began. In doing so, they named their own experiences with heterosexism and homophobia, whether these experiences were having used the words themselves, hearing the words, or having the words used against them. By asking participants to say the words aloud in a group, the Speakers' Bureau asked participants to name and own these experiences in a general, rather than personal, way. The participants were not expected to announce publicly their stances on homosexuality. Rather, they were asked to acknowledge that heterosexism and homophobia are out there in the world and that they have experienced these forms of oppression—not *how* they have experienced them but *that* they have experienced them.

There was never a lack of responses in the brainstorm until a Speakers' Bureau member invited the audience to list terms used to describe a man who is attracted to women or a woman who is attracted to men. Here, there was often a pause, almost as if this were a trick question. Eventually someone usually said "normal" and others said "straight" and "heterosexual." Then, a facilitating youth would point out how many derogatory words there were for people who are lesbian, gay, and bisexual, and how few such words there were for people who were straight. He or she would then explain how that discrepancy points to heterosexism and homophobia in our society. He or she would also talk about each of the words and the history behind those like *faggot* and *dyke*. Rather than correcting the audience, for example, "You say *faggot* but you should say *gay*," they described the history of hate and hurt that comes along with the derogatory term. It was at this point that a Speakers' Bureau member would distribute the glossary that I describe in the previous chapter. This provided alternate, positive language for audience members to consider and encouraged a deeper understanding of how homophobic terms affect their classmates.

The language analysis then led into a Speakers' Bureau member establishing guidelines for the outreach. For example, the youth facilitator often said something like, "For the purpose of this presentation, and we hope beyond this presentation, we will use the terms *lesbian*, *gay*, and *bisexual*. Also, if it's ok with you, we will use the term *straight*."[1] In this way, Speakers' Bureau members took some power over the hateful words and terms. For example, when they talked about the history of hate and hurt behind *faggot*, people were less likely to use the word during the outreach, and, when they did use it, the Speakers' Bureau members had an established guideline to reference: "For the purpose of *this* presentation, we will use the word gay." This control allowed Speakers' Bureau members to challenge and even prevent the use of heterosexist and homophobic language in ways that they were often not able to in other contexts in which these words are used against them. This introductory activity also laid the foundation for Speakers' Bureau members to talk about the ways that heterosexism and homophobia impacted them, as LGBTQ people, and how they coped.

Writing (About) Themselves

Speakers' Bureau members almost always included stories about themselves in their outreach. These stories provided them with opportunities to write themselves into the world of schools, which they shared with teachers and students, in and on their own terms. In general, the stories were about their experiences of coming out, as something-other-than-straight, to themselves, their families, and friends. So often, teachers assumed that none of their students were LGBTQ, and students assumed that they did not know anyone who was LGBTQ. Their assumptions were based on the fact that the LGBTQ people they knew had not come out to them. When people are not in open and honest conversation with LGBTQ people, they do not have the opportunity to learn about the experiences of people who are different than themselves in terms of sexual and gender identities. The stories shared by members of the Speakers' Bureau provided audience members one way of learning about what it meant, at least to these particular youth, to be queer.

The Speakers' Bureau members modified their stories according to their audiences. When they spoke with students, they focused on interactions with peers surrounding their sexual identities and gender expressions. When they spoke with teachers, they talked about their experiences in classrooms. When they spoke with administrators, they included anecdotes about their principals and assistant principals.

Here I focus on two examples of outreach conducted for in-service and pre-service teachers. While this outreach took place in a private-university setting rather than a K–12 setting, often outreach was conducted in elementary or secondary contexts. I highlight this outreach because of the focus on literacy or, more specifically, writing the word and the world (Freire, 1987).

In this outreach to teachers of writing, Chas, an African American gay man, explained to the audience that "for me, writing was my outlet to communicate a lot of feeling that I really couldn't communicate to *any*body else, and um, that was all I had, for a very, very long time." He talked about how he used his writing as a way of making sense of thoughts and feelings that he understood as prohibited, as so wrong that they could not be shared with anyone. In his writing, though, he could be his own, trusted audience. Justine reported a similar purpose to her writing. She said, "I was harassed on a daily basis, um, but my only real outlet for how I felt was through my writing." So, not only did she use her writing as she struggled with her own thoughts and feelings, she also used it as a way of dealing with the homophobia she was experiencing in schools. Writing gave Chas and Justine a way of articulating their thoughts and feelings about being gay and lesbian in worlds that they experienced as homophobic. Chas said, "Writing for me, growing up, basically saved my life." In this context, Chas and Justine did not elaborate on their experiences as victims; instead, they informed writing teachers of the incredible significance of their work in the lives of LGBTQ youth, at least as they experienced it.

In this way, Justine and Chas, as well as other Speakers' Bureau members, conveyed to writing teachers the importance both of writing themselves as queer youth into the world of, in this case, teachers and writing *about* themselves, as queer youth. Recall that Justine is the same young person who, only a year before, was thwarted in her 9th-grade English class with respect to writing about LGBTQ-themed topics. As an individual in school, she was unable to convey the importance of writing about same-sex marriages and the dyke march, but as part of a collective, she was able to explain to a whole group of teachers that such writing was meaningful for her and educative for them.

The Speakers' Bureau's stories taught teachers that it was not enough to give students space to write about being LGBTQ, that the teachers must also protect this space. In another outreach just 6 weeks later for pre-service secondary English teachers, Dara, whom you met in Chapter 2, explained how it was not a simple matter of giving students choice and letting them write about topics pertinent to queer youth. She argued that making such choices was risky for students, so it took more than a space, it took a safe space, or at least a safer space, for students to assert their agency. She talked about a journal she was required to keep in her 11th grade English class. Topics were not assigned, but she knew that her teacher would collect and grade it, so she assumed that her teacher would read it. During this school year, she was "having some problems with the girl that [she] was seeing," and she wrote about them in her journal; but instead of using the girl's name, she used the name *Bob* as a substitute, because, as she said, "I didn't want [the teacher] to see that I was seeing another woman." Dara's sense that this class was not a safe enough space in which to write about her lesbian relationship was confirmed when her classmates were allowed to express their homophobic views. She said,

> There was these girls who decided to do a paper, their term paper on gays in the military. And, they addressed their whole, um, their whole, like, speech to me. And, they were like, "oh, no offense, I just think that they shouldn't be there because there's like close quarters." And it wasn't really based on anything that was um *valid*. It was really based on like *fear*, and, um, I didn't see how my teacher let that go.

Here, Dara conveyed to future educators that for LGBTQ students to find and make a space for themselves, teachers must not be complicit in cultivating homophobia in their classrooms.

Provoking Reflection

At the end of almost all of the outreach events, participants were invited to ask questions about LGBTQ youth, which varied dramatically according to the audience. Speakers' Bureau members had the chance to respond, or not, based on their experiences. Sometimes audience members rejected the Speakers' Bureau through disengagement. For example, I watched a group of principals reading newspapers throughout an entire outreach. Other times they rejected the queer youth speakers through active engagement, expressing disapproval of everything the youth presented. At best, though, audience members asked how they could be better friends, teachers, and administrators of LGBTQ youth. For example, in the outreach to pre-service secondary English teachers, one participant asked:

> If you were to be at school and you were to feel that teachers were supportive, what do you think, what would that look like or what would that be like or what would it feel like or what would they do, do you think?

Another person asked, "What do you think a teacher could do to make it more general and open toward gay and lesbian youth?" And still another said, "If you could each just say one thing that maybe you would want us to think about as a middle school teacher or a high school teacher that we could do." These questions created opportunities for the LGBTQ youth to assert their agency in schools through teachers.

Dara, for example, encouraged intervening in homophobic harassment:

> There's a lot of, kind of, verbal harassment stuff that went on. The faggot-dyke-queer thing. And when the teachers didn't say anything about that and kind of say "that's not OK to say, that's offensive," um, to me, it said that "it's alright that they pick on you. It's OK that if [they] call you a faggot. It's OK that they call you a dyke." And to me, it also said that I wasn't really welcome there, if I was a dyke, or, you know, a lesbian. . . . That kind of thing, that "it's not OK to call people dyke, fag, queer," and, you know, "gay people are welcome here. We want everyone to learn here" kind of thing. Not saying that you agree that gay is right, just "They're welcome here."

She also talked about avoiding heterosexist comments in which students' heterosexuality is assumed, such as, having a teacher say, "So, when you, when you all grow up you're going to get married," and "I know you all have boyfriends," to a class of girls. As a part of the Speakers' Bureau, Dara could tell teachers some of the things that teachers did to harm her educational experience and offer suggestions of things they could do to protect their current and future LGBTQ students.

Kira asked for more proactive efforts. She said,

> It would have been great if we read books just by, about gay people in the school. . . . It would make it easier for me to learn if I had images of myself in my class. I would have been drawn in. I would have been right there.

She talked about how her teachers would give full biographies of some authors, but when it came to gay authors, like Walt Whitman, they would not say anything about their sexual identities. She said that she wished teachers would "just mention it, you don't have to have a three-hour class on it. Just mentioning it would have been great. But not, sometimes they even just skipped over it, you know." Here, Dara and Kira reflected on their experiences with teachers in schools and challenged these teachers to do more for their LGBTQ students.

One of the teachers, a middle school English teacher in the local school district, commented:

> You said something that really struck me. I just think about my own practice in the classroom and how much I personally love Langston Hughes, and whenever I teach Langston Hughes I've never mentioned to my students that he was gay. And, um, and even thinking about doing that now, I have to think about a lot of other things in terms of parents and administrators and how I would frame that and present it, what it would mean after saying it. But just reflecting on the fact that I've never done that is very interesting to me.

This teacher saw that she protected herself from potentially homophobic parents and administrators, even though she would only have been "guilty" of homosexuality by proxy, and perhaps she protected their homophobia as well. However, she was not trying to protect LGBTQ students when she failed to acknowledge Langston Hughes as a gay man. Thus, the dialogue in the outreach served to provoke reflection that had the potential of making space for LGBTQ youth in schools through literacy performances.

Speakers' Bureau members, as a collective, worked to make space for LGBTQ youth in schools by analyzing language, writing about themselves as LGBTQ youth, (re)writing themselves into the world of school, and provoking reflection among students and teachers. By talking about terms and the histories of hate and hurt behind those terms with teachers and students, Speakers' Bureau members laid the groundwork for further reflection on the words they have used, or heard people use, and the ways in which they have responded, or not, to the use of such words. This reflection opened up the possibility of change. For example, having learned about the impact of such terms, people may be less likely to use them and may be more likely to intervene when others use them. When Speakers' Bureau members told their personal stories, they had opportunities to articulate to people in schools what they wanted, and needed, as queer youth in schools. In this way, these young people worked to create a safe-enough space, if not for themselves, for others like them, at least with regard to sexual identities and gender expressions, to write themselves into the worlds of schools. By inviting participants to ask questions and responding to these questions based on their own experiences, Speakers' Bureau members had opportunities to bring their insights to the curiosities of the participants and to instigate reflection by those participants to create a dialogue. This work of Speakers' Bureau members at outreach events not only educated participants in ways that hold the potential to make space for LGBTQ youth in schools, it also helped them to assert agency to work within and against a system, in this case a school system, that is in many ways quite resistant to such work.

PRACTITIONER APPLICATIONS: PROMOTE STUDENT ACTIVISM

Following the example of the Speakers' Bureau, teachers and youth service providers can help students in their classrooms and youth in their programs to analyze language, to write about themselves, and to provoke reflection around issues related to homophobia. Moreover, they can promote student activism in the following ways:

- Speak kind words to outsiders; listen.
- Recognize reading and writing as having life-saving potential for some—but not all—young people.
- Co-create a safe-enough space for and with marginalized students; protect this space.
- Educate students and colleagues about equity and diversity issues; provoke reflection around issues of oppression; analyze hate-based language with students; provide related resources.
- Be a part of designing and implementing equity and diversity policies.

- Help students construct their interests in ways suitable for school.
- Take student efforts at activism seriously; support them.

One can imagine these suggestions directed specifically toward LGBTQQ people or about any other marginalized population.

Together, the chapters of the second section build an argument for LGBTQQ youth as agents and activists, effectively rejecting the notion of LGBTQQ youth only as victims. The third section shifts focus to what student and teacher allies do and can do on behalf of LGBTQQ youth.

Part III

STUDENTS AND TEACHERS AS ALLIES

LGBTQQ youth use literacy as a tool to develop and assert their agency in a world that is often heterosexist, even if not homophobic. The impact of their efforts increases infinitely when combined with the effort of allies.

According to the Gay, Lesbian and Straight Education Network (GLSEN), "allies generally are non-LGBT people who are committed to ending bias and discrimination against LGBT people," but they can be "anyone who supports ending anti-LGBT name-calling, bullying and harassment. . . . For instance, a bisexual adult can be an ally to LGBT students, and a lesbian student can be an ally to a transgender student" (http://www.allyweek.org/about/index.cfm).[1]

People learn, in both overt and subtle ways, values. But in many U.S. communities the implicit lessons related to LGBTQQ people are heterosexist and homophobic ones. To learn the values associated with being an ally requires more explicit teaching.

So, how do people learn to become and be allies? With this question in mind, I turn to examples of a teacher inquiry and a literature discussion group. When I do so, you will notice that I do so in chapters entitled "be(com)ing" either teacher or student allies. I recognize that this structure is awkward, but I use it deliberately to draw attention to how the two, both becoming and being, are infinitely reciprocal. It is not chronological as "becoming and being" suggests. Just as an LGBTQQ person does not get to come out once and for all but must come out over and over again to different people at different times in different places and in different ways, an ally cannot be an ally by a single declaration. It is not as if one declares one's self an ally and then relaxes in self-congratulations. Instead, an ally must perform being an ally repeatedly, and what an ally performance looks like in one space, perhaps at home, is different than it is in another, say, at school. Moreover, what one LGBTQQ person experiences as support is different than what another might experience as support. Learning what these infinite ally performances might look like is an endless process. One must constantly work on becoming an ally in order to be one at all. This was evident in both the teacher inquiry group as well as the related literature discussion group.

The teacher inquiry group was started by Jim Buckley, Caroline Clark, Jeane Copenhaver-Johnson, and me—a gay man, two straight allies, and a lesbian. Our goal was to combat heterosexism and homophobia in classrooms and schools. Members of the group, like the founders, included gay men, straight women and men, and lesbians, although most of the group members were straight women (Blackburn, Clark, Kenney, & Smith, 2010). The literature discussion group emerged from the teacher inquiry group, as teachers brought together some of their students to talk about LGBTQ-themed literature (Blackburn, 2008; Blackburn & Clark, 2011; Clark & Blackburn, 2009).

In Chapter 4, I talk about the literature discussion group. The group's conversations reveal how students draw on their readings of LGBTQ-themed texts to become allies both in queer friendly contexts, like our discussions, and in less-queer-friendly contexts, like schools. In Chapter 5, I turn to the teacher inquiry group. An exploration of our work together shows how teachers, particularly teachers of the English language arts, advocate on behalf of LGBTQQ youth through the work of making space for these young people in schools.

Overall, the third section shifts focus from the agency and activism of LGBTQQ youth to the advocacy and activist work of student allies and teacher allies. In doing so, it reminds readers that all of us, not just LGBTQQ youth, can work against heterosexism and homophobia in classrooms and schools. Moreover, it offers concrete examples of how some people accomplish this work, particularly in ways that engage literacy performances.

4

Be(com)ing Student Allies

Over the course of 3 years a group of young people and their teachers, both LGBTQQ and ally, met together to discuss LGBTQ-themed books. The group met in Kaleidoscope Youth Center, a center for LGBTQ youth in Columbus, Ohio. My colleague Caroline Clark and I participated in and documented the group's 20 meetings. Adult participants, including Caroline and me, included 6 allies, 3 lesbians, and 1 gay male. Youth participants included 11 allies, 7 gay males, 3 lesbians, and 2 female-to-male transgender youth who were attracted to females. For the purpose of this chapter, I focus on student allies.

Over time, I was struck by the ways that youth learned how to advocate on behalf of LGBTQQ people through our readings and discussion of LGBTQ-themed texts. I was also interested in the distinct ways they were already advocates among LGBTQQ youth in the literature discussion group in contrast to their ways of being at home and school. Perhaps what stood out to me most was how it seemed that the only way for the young people to *be* allies was by always *becoming* allies. Selecting, reading, and discussing LGBTQ-themed texts holds great potential in the endless becoming of allies, but its potential would increase exponentially if it were fostered in schools.

BECOMING ALLIES THROUGH READING

People can learn to become allies by selecting, reading, and discussing LGBTQ-themed literature in part because these stories can teach readers something about the experiences of LGBTQQ people, but also because this literature can provide images of allies and, thus, opportunities to consider the impact of their actions.

In the literature discussion group, for example, Rebecca, a White ally, learned a bit about the history of gay men when we read and discussed Newman's (1988) "A Letter to Harvey Milk." The short story is about Harry, an elderly Jewish man, who confronts some of his experiences with Jewish gay men, including Harvey Milk, as he comes to know his creative writing teacher as a Jewish lesbian. The teacher has a pink triangle pin on her backpack. Because this symbol was used by Nazis to identify gay men in concentration camps during the Holocaust, it conjures for Harry memories of his experiences in a concentration camp, which he writes about for their class. Rebecca was previously unaware of the history of the pink triangle. In our discussion of this story, she said, "I just found it shocking. Because I never knew about the upside down pink triangle thing. I never knew about that, and I was like . . . I was like, whoa. It was eye-opening. I was like, wow." Not only was this history new to Rebecca, it was one that she found appalling. Moreover, she learned about it in a context in which she could express her shock and communicate her support for gay people without homophobic repercussions. Thus, she positioned herself as an ally.

Most often, young people do not learn these histories at all. When they do, they are sometimes assumed, by their ally teachers, to be homophobes rather than allies. Therefore the implicit goal is to elicit sympathy or pity rather than reflection and support. This kind of learning about homophobia is evident in studies involving a single LG-themed text being read and discussed in an English language arts class or lesson (Athanases, 1996; Carey-Webb, 2001; Epstein, 2000; Greenbaum, 1994; Hamilton, 1998; Hoffman, 1993; Schall & Kauffmann, 2003). Other times, youth learn about homophobia when they are being punished for their homophobic behavior. Gonzales (2010), for example, writes about explaining to his student what he understood to be the derivation (he later questioned this explanation) of the word *fag* as coming from the word *faggot*, meaning a bundle of sticks, in reference to the practice of burning at the stake men who were thought to be homosexual. He offered this explanation essentially as punishment for a student who continued to use the epithet. Gonzales' approach, that is more punitive than educative, is not a unique one; but his reflection on it as a problematic approach is worth considering.

Let me be clear: I understand that the approaches of Rebecca and Gonzales came from a place of genuine desire to combat homophobia through inclusion and intervention, respectively. And it is not that either of these approaches is wrong. Instead, I hope that more teachers will include LGBTQ-themed texts in their curriculum, even in homophobic classrooms and schools, and I advocate for teachers addressing homophobia when they hear it. Still, both of these approaches set up antagonistic dynamics between the ally teacher and the homophobic students. I am not trying to pretend that most students are not homophobic but to argue that homophobia is neither a permanent state of being nor a state that is independent of context. In other words, people are not simply homophobes or allies. They may perform homophobic behavior sometimes in some contexts and not in others. It is understandable that in places such as schools, where gender rules and regulations are enforced so intensely, people are more likely to perform homophobic behaviors. For this reason, it is worth looking to more queer friendly contexts for lessons on performing ally behavior that might then be applied to schools. (For more on this relationship, see Blackburn, 2007.)

Just as selecting, reading, and discussing LGBTQ-themed literature helps young allies understand the experiences, and in the above case, history of gay people, it also provides opportunities for youth allies to examine straight characters' actions and reflect on the consequences of their actions, particularly with respect to LGBTQQ people. More specifically, allies can consider whether characters are or are not behaving in ways that support LGBTQQ characters. In other words, they can study what it takes to be an ally. For example, when the literature discussion group talked about *Boy Meets Boy* (Levithan, 2003), Mary, a White straight ally, pointed to a scene in which the main character goes with a group of friends to the house of another character to pick him up for a date. In her words, "Paul came up [to pick up another boy for a date] and [the date's parent] was like, 'are you his date?' and then everybody stepped in and like, 'we're all his dates,' and they all just jumped in the car." So Mary, a straight ally, interpreted the friends as good allies because they stood up with Paul.

Having such discussions among LGBTQQ people is beneficial to allies because they can listen to and learn from LGBTQQ people what they experience as supportive. For example, in our discussion of *The God Box* (Sanchez, 2007), Laura, a Jewish lesbian, found the actions of the straight father of the gay main character, both Latino, particularly inspiring. She directed us to a scene in which the father stood up for his son in their church's congregation to rebut the minister's homophobic message. She said that this scene "really moved" her because "it was so sweet, and just right." In this way, Laura, as a lesbian, conveyed to her ally peers her understanding of the significance of an ally explicitly and publicly supporting an LGBTQQ person, a message that might be difficult to deliver in a more homophobic context.

In this group, ally and LGBTQQ youth also talked together to construct what a good ally might do, as is evident in the discussion of *The Perks of Being a Wallflower* (Chbosky, 1999). This novel is written through a series of letters to an unnamed person from Charlie. Charlie is a kind and generous protagonist, and the book chronicles a period in high school in which he makes good friends, falls in love with a girl, and comes to recall and process his traumatic past. One of his good friends is Patrick. In one part of the book, Patrick's boyfriend rejects him because of his internalized homophobia, and Patrick is drunk and sad. Charlie is trying to console him and, in this moment, Patrick kisses Charlie. We discussed this scene:

> *Mollie* (lesbian adult): I liked when he and Patrick kissed and Charlie didn't like panic about it or whatever. So I liked—
> *Alice* (youth ally): He kissed him back.
> *Mollie*: Yeah, and that was good.
> *Anna* (youth ally): I like how he was so comfortable with it.
> *Debbie* (adult ally): He's comfortable.
> *Mollie*: Yeah.
> *Isaac* (gay youth): I did like the fact that—
> *Anna*: It didn't matter to him.

And then later, in the same discussion, I asked the group what they thought about Patrick kissing Charlie, and Melissa, a youth ally, stated, "I think Charlie was just kind of letting Patrick, it's his friend, so he was just kind of just saying that because he was trying to help him feel better, so he just let him." Together, we talked about how we appreciated the image of an ally who responds to a romantic move by his same-sex friend not with fear but with ease and empathy. This stands in stark contrast to the more often heard, "I don't care if you're gay, as long as you don't hit on me."

We also talked together about actions that were not supportive, for example, in our discussion of *Two Parties, One Tux, and a Very Short Film about* The Grapes of Wrath (Goldman, 2008). In this novel, Mitchell is the main character, and his best friend David comes out as gay. As Mitchell struggles to be a good friend to David, Mitchell's sister begins to suspect that Mitchell is gay. As a result, she reads a letter from David to Mitchell, which disconfirms her suspicion. Although the sister is somewhat like-able, the group points to two of her actions that are not what we thought a good ally would do. First, I talked with a lesbian and a gay youth about her reading the letter:

> *Lisa*: Didn't she like pry, though?
> *Travis*: Yeah, she was very persistent.
> *Mollie*: Didn't she read the letter?!

Here, the three of us called into question the sister's role as an ally. Implied in our discussion is that a good ally doesn't invade one's privacy but waits to be told, even if what is being told was long suspected. Then, in the con-versation, a youth ally continued along these lines. Rebecca said, quoting Mitchell in reference to his sister, "She was so excited that I might be gay. I think I disappointed her." Here Rebecca problematized the sister's being excited about the opportunity to be an ally as a move that foregrounds the ally's goodness rather than the support that person might offer to an LGBTQQ person. In other words, Rebecca's interpretation suggested that a good ally doesn't focus on how good they are as much as what they can offer to support an LGBTQQ person.

The group developed, over time, a less dichotomous notion of good ally and bad ally. This was evident in our final meeting when we talked about *Prayers for Bobby* (Aarons, 1995), a journalistic biography of a straight mother, Mary, whose gay son, Bobby, ultimately committed suicide at least in part due to her constant disapproval grounded in her fundamentalist interpretations of the Bible. Still, Melissa, an ally youth, and Jack, a gay youth, grappled with how to make sense of Mary in ally terms, a quite generous move, I think:

> *Melissa*: I don't think Mary was as bad as [Mary's] mom was because [Mary] still loved her son. She was harsh, but I think because of her mother, she had the constant fear that her son would go to hell because what he's doing is a sin, but I think if she had not been raised like that, and if her mother had not used the excuse that God's watching you, just to make her behave, she would have
>
> *Jack*: I forgave Mary at the end because she didn't forgive herself. Because she knew that, I mean she said in the speech that it was a direct result of his parents not loving, or you know, not showing the love. And that's why at the end I grew to like her a lot because she, I mean she realized that, and, you can, I mean, I'm not sure whether you can blame her or not because of what you said, [how] she was raised, the way that she did feel about things, but the fact that she recognized that that was wrong and then changed and not only changed but became active in the opposite. I really, really liked it.

Here Melissa and Jack talked together about the complexity of being an ally, particularly how it is not that one is or isn't an ally, but rather that one might have serious, understandable, almost insurmountable obstacles to becoming an ally and still perform ally behavior in time.

BEING ALLIES

Another way of becoming allies is *through the being of allies*, that is, practicing the behaviors that are intended and experienced as support by LGBTQQ

people. Being an ally looks different for different people in different contexts. Below, I discuss what straight allies did to support LGBTQQ people in
queer friendly contexts and in less friendly ones, such as home and school.

In Queer Friendly Contexts

In the literature discussion group, ally students practiced their roles as
allies, which prepared them to be stronger advocates in more challenging,
or more homophobic, contexts. An example is our discussion of *Finding
H. F.*, a novel set in rural Kentucky about H. F., who is coming out as a lesbian, and Bo, her gay best friend. Bo's father is overtly homophobic. Melissa,
a biracial youth ally, talked about how difficult it must be for Bo. She said,

> [The book] talks about how Bo's dad used to be a logger until he hurt
> his back and all that, he's a drinker and he has . . . I underlined that
> because I was thinking of how hard it must be for Bo, like because
> he's gay but I don't think he can say anything to his dad, the only
> one he can tell, except for H. F. . . . . It's hard for her too but I don't
> think it would be as hard for her as it is for him.

Here, Melissa pushes herself to understand the complexities of LGBTQQ
people and their varied experiences with homophobia. In doing so, Melissa positioned herself as an ally of LGBTQQ people by reflecting on and
responding empathically to lesbian and gay characters.

Another way that youth allies supported LGBTQQ people through
their reading and discussions was by being open to broad interpretations
of desire beyond that that is experienced between straight men and wom-
en. For example, we read back-to-back *The Color Purple* (Walker, 1982) and
Fried Green Tomatoes at the Whistle Stop Café (Flagg, 1987). *The Color Purple* is
a Pulitzer-Prize-winning epistolary novel focused on the roles of African
American women in rural Georgia in the 1930s. It is written as a series of
letters and journal entries by sisters Celie and Nettie. *Fried Green Tomatoes*
is also set in the rural south during the depression era; it focuses on the
relationship between two White women, Idgie and Ruth. When discussing these two novels, questions were raised about the sexuality of Shug in
the former and Eva in the latter. We understood both female characters to
have sexual and romantic relationships with men and at least one woman
(Shug with Celie and Eva with Idgie). In talking about these characters,
Sarah, a White youth ally, suggested that Shug and Eva were "open-mind-
ed" when it came to desire and that they "just love love." This suggestion
suspends classification by avoiding categorizing the characters as bisexual, for example, and focusing on desire in ways that are not restricted by
the genders of those experiencing it.

Moreover, straight allies do not show repulsion or even resistance when that affection is turned toward them, much like how Charlie responded to Patrick's kiss in *The Perks of Being a Wallflower*. This was also the case within our group. For example, Melissa and Isaac talked about two female classmates who expressed physical affection for Melissa quite freely, even though she had a boyfriend and identified as straight. Melissa acknowledged that she was misinterpreted as lesbian as a result, but she did not seem disturbed by either the affection or being read as homosexual.

In a queer friendly context, as the literature discussion group was, being an ally meant openly learning about LGBTQQ people and their histories and being understanding of same-sex desire. Although such performances of ally behavior are typically more modest in less-queer-friendly contexts, such overt ally behavior provides a significant foundation from which to work in places like home and school.

At Home

Several of the group participants were siblings of lesbian and gay people. These young people may have been uniquely positioned to engage in ally work in their homes in that they may have felt more compelled to make their homes queer friendly than other ally peers, while they also were less at risk than their LGBTQQ peers. Melissa, for example, had a lesbian sister who was out to some of their family but not to their grandmother:

> My sister, she's like, she has a girlfriend, she's like out but not to my grandma. So we're like, oh, and we were laughing and making fun of my sister because my sister went to Times Square in New York [with her girlfriend]. And we're like, "What if grandma sees you on New Year's Eve? Calls us up and says, 'I saw Jacqueline on TV.'"

Even though Melissa recognized her grandmother's discomfort with lesbian and gay people, she asserted her ally identity with her. She told this story in the literature discussion group:

> *Melissa*: Yeah, my grandmother, she was like, because I told her I had to stay after school to talk about GSA, she was like, "What is GSA?" And my brother was like, "You know grandma's not going to know that." I told her what it was, and she said, "Why do they have that in the schools?" because she didn't understand because she's all religious.
> *Debbie*: And how did she respond?

Mollie: I think you were brave to tell her.
Melissa: She was like, I don't know, she was just like kind of like confused and weird about it.

Melissa used her association with her school's Gay Straight Alliance to assert an ally identity in her home. This was a difficult move, as evidenced by the disapproval it conjured, which Melissa was not obligated to face and could have avoided. Her actions, however, laid a bit of groundwork for the possibility that one day Jacqueline might come out to their grandmother.

Rebecca also had a sister who was a lesbian. She was out to her mother, but her mother was not very accepting of homosexuality. Rebecca reported having watched the movie version of a book we read and discussed: *Prayers for Bobby* (Mulcahy, 2009). As I mentioned previously, this book reports on a mother shifting from homophobe to ally as she comes to terms with the suicide of her gay son. Rebecca talked about watching this movie with her mother and how both of them cried. Rebecca challenged her mother's lack of acceptance of Rebecca's sister by forcing her to consider the possible consequences for her rejection. This cautionary tale conjured intense emotion, perhaps empathy, perhaps guilt or even fear, from her mother and perhaps laid the groundwork for change.

Through literacy performances, Melissa and Rebecca challenged authority figures in their homes at least to acknowledge that someone they knew was an ally and at best to acknowledge that their homophobia negatively impacted someone they love.

In School

Being allies at school is a different sort of challenge in part because one's teachers, unlike parents or guardians, change so frequently. With each new teacher, students must come to know the teachers' values that will help shape the experience of the class as well as the school. Therefore, students have to pay close attention to the roles teachers play in fostering or combating homophobia in classrooms and schools. Anna, a biracial youth ally, talked about this in relationship to her move from middle school to high school. Initially, she thought middle school and high school were really different in regard to what she called "the gay thing" in that it was "forbidden" by teachers in middle school and "okay" with teachers in high school. But, she was not so sure any more because she had witnessed so many teachers ignoring homophobic behaviors. She said,

Anna: Some teachers, I'm not going to name them, but they'll hear the word like *gay* [as an epithet], like I constantly hear the word just thrown around, like all the time.

Jeff: Like *gay* and *faggot*.
Anna: They hear it like right in front of them and they don't say a word.

Based on Anna and Jeff's accounts, teachers fostered homophobia in schools by failing to intervene. Noticing the role teachers play in fostering homophobia is important work in being an ally in schools. One cannot work against homophobia if one does not pay attention to how it gets produced and allowed.

It is just as important to bring focus to these observations by identifying which teachers foster what sorts of contexts. Anna, for example, critiqued one of her teachers, Mr. Peterson, for engaging with one of his students about whether another student was gay. She said,

Anna: Someone called Jerome gay and Mr. Peterson was just like, he looked at them, like the person who said it, and then he was like [nodded yes]. . .
Mollie: He nodded yes to suggest that like "yes he is gay"?
Anna: Like he was like, he wasn't exactly like, "yeah, like right on." He was like, "ooh," and then he continued his work.

She suggested that the teacher expressed interest in knowing whether Jerome was gay rather than addressing the fact that students were characterizing him as gay in a derogatory manner. This is the same teacher, the same class, and even the same young person from Anna's story in Chapter 1, in which both boys were punished when John called Jerome a "fucking faggot."

When Anna told this story in the group, Jeff had an intense reaction to the mere mention of John. He said, "I hate that kid [John]. One of these days he's going to get hit by a bus and I'm going to be the driver." This reaction was generally uncharacteristic of Jeff, but similar to one he exhibited a few other times, all of which were when he was reacting to overtly homophobic behaviors, both in life and texts. His reaction revealed what I understand to be the real threat that John and other homophobic students posed for him as a gay student in this school. John could have done to Jeff what Anna reported he did to Jerome, that is make him vulnerable by publicly naming him a "fucking faggot," regardless of how the boys actually identified.

Anna recognized Mr. Peterson's lack of action against homophobia as a problem. Her ability to solve the problem was hindered, though, by her fear of, as she said earlier, "get[ting] in trouble." Thus, Mr. Peterson not only allowed homophobic behavior, he also prevented ally behavior.

It is just as important for student allies to notice what teachers do to combat homophobia in schools, even if these examples are much less, well, noticeable. Melissa, who went to school with Anna and Jeff, asked, vaguely, "Didn't one of the teachers say, get on a kid for like, you know saying like, talking bad about gays or something?" No one answered her question, so she said, "Someone was like saying something about gays, and [the teacher] said, 'alright, alright, enough is enough.'" Recognizing the relative lack of risk this teacher took, Debbie, an ally teacher at the school, asked, perhaps rhetorically, "Well did he address it or did he just say, 'alright, alright, that's enough.' Do you remember?" Not exactly answering Debbie's question, but helping Melissa make her point, Anna said, "He didn't raise his voice, but like people stopped after he said it." For ally students, this intervention, albeit minimal, was worth recognition, particularly in contrast to Mr. Peterson.

In the example Melissa shared, a teacher, because of his authority, could make a rather small move to interrupt homophobic behavior, even if only temporarily. In Anna's example, though, a student who actively identified as an ally and participated in the school's GSA felt unable to make a similar move in a comparable situation or even report the event to an ally teacher. I asked the youth about what I understood to be ally vulnerability in schools. Anna explained that one of the risks of being an ally was being misunderstood as LGBTQQ and therefore vulnerable to homophobia. She said,

> I myself am straight and I attend the GSA meetings, I read the [LGBTQ-themed] books and I'm not afraid to be part of GSA because, and the name says Gay *Straight* Alliance. And they just kind of see the gay part and just automatically assume there's all gay people inside of it. And I was reading this book and one of my friends asked, "Anna are you gay, are you bi or–" "I'm perfectly straight."

I asked her, then, why she was willing to be an ally in school, and she plainly stated, "I just think that everyone's equal, and I support everyone."

Additionally, their straight ally teacher, Debbie, claimed that people like Anna participating in the GSA improved the status of the club by disrupting the stereotypes that, in Isaac's words, GSAs are "dating service[s]" or that they host "make-out sessions" or "orgies" for same-sex couples. Debbie said,

> To give credit to the students, I think you've changed a lot of [the stereotypes associated with GSA], like they know Anna and they know Melissa and Jeff, you know. Well they know who you are and that's changing [the stereotypes].

In addition to disrupting stereotypes, Anna claimed that her being an active ally in school provoked others to be allies as well:

> *Anna*: It's really interesting because I'm like the school president of the freshmen class and I'm in GSA so people are like, like pretty much like everyone knows me and they know I'm in GSA so they're thinking like, I don't know, just like . . .
>
> *Jeane* (adult ally): Or that it makes it more appealing. I was thinking maybe it would make it more appealing.
>
> *Anna*: Yeah, like they always ask about it and if it's fun, it interests a lot of people.

Because Anna had social capital in her school, as evidenced by her status as class president, her role as an ally drew other people into the role. So, according to Anna, allies risk vulnerability associated with being an ally because they believe it is the right thing to do and, according to Debbie, because it disrupts stereotypes of GSAs and again, according to Anna, because being allies can increase the impact of their efforts by drawing other people into the work. In other words, allies risk vulnerability to combat homophobia because it matters.

Group members reported that there were times when reading books for our discussion group instigated homophobic behavior from peers, which, in turn, demanded ally behavior. We talked about this particularly after reading our first book, *Boy Meets Boy* (Levithan, 2003). As you may recall from Chapter 1, the book's title and cover call attention to the fact that this is a book about gay people, and Jeff described how reading it in science class provoked homophobic comments. Anna had a similar experience as an ally. Her friend Craig said he didn't even want to touch the book since it was about gay characters. One might imagine that these students would stop reading LGBTQ-themed books, stop coming to the group, or just stop reading these books at school. And, as I mentioned earlier, the second book they selected had a more subdued gay theme, and also had a title and cover that in no way suggests this theme. Even so, ultimately, the youth returned to reading obviously LGBTQ-themed books. Anna, for example, reported reading *Fun Home* (Bechdel, 2006) in school. Although the title and cover do not reveal that it is a lesbian-themed text, it becomes obvious to people around the reader because the book is a graphic novel that includes, among many other images, a sex scene between two women. Anna and her teacher Debbie talk about Anna's reading this segment of the book in their school:

> *Debbie*: And of course Anna is reading it when, you know, the ladies are together alone, in school.

Anna: Oh God, I was reading the intimate parts and I was in school,
and I was like done with my exam, and I was like
[unidentifiable participant]: Right because the pictures . . .
Mollie: Oh that's funny. Because I was thinking about how these
covers don't really reveal anything about the content of the book.
. . . And I was thinking about the pictures themselves, they really
do. Right, right. Did anybody ask you about the book?
Anna: My friend Ned actually, he was like, "What are you reading?"
And I was like, this book for book club. He was like, "Oh that's
cool." And I was like right, almost to the part, and he was like,
"Whoa, what's this?" And I was like, "um, book club."

While reading visibly LGBTQ-themed texts in less-queer-friendly
contexts is clearly a risk, it is also an act that accomplishes the literacy
performances of identifying publicly as an ally. This disrupts the perhaps unarticulated assumption that all people share homophobic values.
Moreover, a visible ally, particularly one with social capital, invites other
people to join in ally work. In many ways, it is difficult to be an ally in
schools and other homophobic contexts. There are few curricular opportunities to learn about LGBTQQ people and their histories. Conveying
openness to same-sex desire and challenging public acts of homophobia
come with great penalties. Alternatively, participating in GSAs and reading visibly LGBTQ-themed texts in school seem to be possibilities for
asserting ally identities.

BEING ALLIES BY ALWAYS BECOMING ALLIES

Working with ally students, as well as with ally teachers, as I discuss in
the next chapter, has helped me to think about allies in terms of performa-
tivity (Butler, 1999). That is, the most effective way of being an ally is by
always becoming an ally.

As discussed in prior sections, allies need to learn about LGBTQQ
people by engaging in educative discussions with LGBTQQ people about
queer-related topics. For example, after we selected and read *The Tragedy
of Miss Geneva Flowers* (Babcock, 2002), but before we discussed it as a
group, Anna was struck, in her reading of the book by its portrayal of
promiscuity—particularly, concealed promiscuity—among gay men, specifically, gay White men. Rather than make assumptions about this population, Anna asked a gay, White male friend about the accuracy of this
representation. Her friend confirmed the stereotype, from his perspective,
drawing on his own experiences of trying to develop relationships with
men who seem only to be interested in sexual encounters.

Anna's report of this conversation led the group to talk about why this might be the case. Alice hypothesized that gay men engaged in frequent anonymous sex as a way of coping in a homophobic society. She said, "You have to hide relationships so like that they won't last long because they'll hide it and it'll get out and they'll have to find someone else." In other words, it is better to have anonymous sex, because it can be concealed more easily than an ongoing relationship. Just as Anna was genuinely motivated to figure out the accuracy of the representation of gay men as engaging in frequent anonymous sex, Alice was motivated to understand why gay men might do this. Unlike Anna though, Alice drew from her own experiences rather than those of a gay man. She said, "You know the parks they have . . . like where the guys meet up in the car . . . I was driving and there were just these guys, there were probably twelve of them just in their cars," and ultimately concluded that this behavior "was odd but it's sad that they have to hide out." Up to this point in the conversation, Alice had not looked to LGBTQQ people to try to develop her understanding and, as a result, had come to a place of pity rather than empathy.

Later in the same conversation, though, it was Alice who sought information from a gay man in the group. Jeff, a gay White male, said that it was difficult for him to conceal the "flamboyancy" in his voice, and Alice wanted to know more:

Alice: Have you talked like that since you were a kid?
Jeff: Yeah.
Alice: Like you really can't help it?
Jeff: Yeah.
Alice: That's awesome.

If you understand her response, "That's awesome," as an attempt to give Jeff a sense of confidence in his voice, it was weak. If, however, you interpret it as a way of communicating that her questions came from a place of respect rather than critique, it was fairly effective. The latter interpretation seems viable to me, considering how the conversation continued.

Jeff went on to explain how it was so difficult for him, in his words, to "have to hide my voice" that "sometimes I don't even talk. I just let people say whatever they want." Caroline, an adult ally, asked when and where he felt like he had to hide his voice, and Jeff said, "Church. In church. I was dragged to church every day by my foster parents. They just hated the fact that I would speak the way I did or do whatever I did because they were strict Catholics." Again, Alice sought more information:

Alice: Did they think the church would like cure you?
Jeff: Yeah, that's what they thought.

Alice: Oh God.

Jeff: They always had me repent my sins every day.

In this brief interaction, Alice sought information from a gay man about what it's like to be a gay man and ultimately communicated her *empathy*, when she said, "Oh God," as distinct from *pity*. It was not that she wasn't an ally at the beginning of this meeting of the literature discussion group and was at the end of it. Rather, it's that she was being an ally by striving to become one throughout the meeting, and in this case, by engaging in educative discussions with LGBTQQ people about queer-related topics, such as conversion efforts from straight guardians with respect to a gay youth.

In such literature discussions, allies can learn about diversity within groups of LGBTQQ people as well. Isaac, for example, in our discussion of ally-authored *Erik & Isabelle: Sophomore Year at Foresthill High* (Wallace, 2005), pointed out to the group the overly simplistic representation of gay men in the book. He said, "All the gay guys in the book are extreme jocks." This prompted a discussion among members about the various gay males in the book, in which an adult ally said, "Well, they are all buff," and I responded, "They're gorgeous and perfect." The ally agreed, saying, "That's true," and later, "Like they all work out and look great." Then Isaac, making his point about not all gay men being the same, said, "Obviously *I* do not work out." Anna, a youth ally, ultimately picked up on the critique by recognizing a different stereotype that the author perpetuated. She pointed out that when the author portrays a gay man as something other than a jock, he is still gorgeous and perfect, but instead of being a jock, he is an artist. Through this discussion, Isaac used his experiences as a gay man to critique this ally-authored book and, thus, provided allies in the group with opportunities to critique overly simplistic, even when positive, representations of gay men in literature.

Moreover, and more importantly, in such discussions, allies can reflect on and struggle with their own efforts as allies, with the additional insights of LGBTQQ people. Melissa, for example, in our discussion of *The God Box*, posed one of the dilemmas she encountered as an ally to the group. She said,

> Today at lunch, actually, we got on the topic of gay marriage, and how Rebecca and I were talking about how we really wanted to see it come about like everywhere while we were still alive because of our sisters [who are lesbians]. And, one girl at our lunch table said, she's like, "I have no problem with gay people, but I just can't see a man and a man or a woman and a woman because marriage is between a man and a woman," and she has no problems with gays or anything,

but she's got that like imbedded in her mind because it's what she's been taught, and she can't let go of it. She wasn't trying to be mean or defensive or anything, she was just being honest, like that she couldn't see it, she couldn't grasp it, and understand it.

Upon reflection, I understand Melissa as genuinely wanting to be a good friend, sister, and ally and sincerely grappling with how to synthesize all of those roles. At the time, I was fully involved in the account and thinking about how I wanted to respond to the girl, or perhaps more accurately, how I wished Melissa had responded to the girl. After some discussion, I said,

> People who say that, like want to distinguish civil unions and marriage, feel just as warm and welcoming to me as love-the-sinner-hate-the-sin people. Like what it feels to me, like, is like I appreciate the honesty, and I hear your comment about being honest and not trying to be mean or defensive or anything like that, it just feels to me ignorant. Like you don't know you're hurting me, so *you* feel better about it, but *I* feel worse about it.

My diatribe provoked the following interaction:

> *Melissa*: The girl said, "I don't have a problem recognizing it as a union, you just can't call it marriage," like she just couldn't give that name to it.
> *Mollie*: Yeah.
> *Melissa*: Like she could see it as they're together, their union.
> *Mollie*: Right, right.
> *Melissa*: But she just couldn't call it marriage.
> *Mollie*: Right. And that feels the same to me as, you know, "You can sit on the back of the bus." [And I'm supposed to be like,] "Thanks, we can be on the same bus."
> *Laura*: That's totally what it is.

Although we, as a group, were never able to provide Melissa with the right answer of how to respond to the girl, we were able to convey to her how Laura and I, as lesbians, experienced the girl's stance. We thus educated her about the consequences of such a stance, on at least some LGBTQ people.

The point is not that LGBTQQ people need to be positioned constantly as educators of allies. That would become miserable for everyone involved. Rather, it is that allies learn to monitor themselves with a consciousness of how what they do and say impacts LGBTQQ populations. Anna, for example, told the group about how people often assumed that she was lesbian because she was in the school's GSA. She said,

> It's like I'm straight and the people are like, "Oh you're in that GSA thing, you're a lesbian." And I'm like, "No I'm not" and then I feel like I have to let them know that I'm not, but I shouldn't have to.

Caroline then asked her how she felt about this, and Anna explained, "I feel bad, like if I'm like, 'No I'm not gay,' like I feel like I was letting down the people that are gay in the group . . . because it really shouldn't matter, but it does, right." Anna had thought through how her response to some of her peers' assumptions that she was a lesbian would impact not only herself but also her LGBTQQ classmates.

Thus, in collaboration, allies and LGBTQQ youth co-constructed what it might look like for a character, an author, and themselves to be allies through their selection, reading, and discussion of LGBTQ-themed books. Consider what it might be like to be in a classroom and school, as a teacher or student who is questioning his/her sexuality or who has just had a family member come out to him/her. Now, think about what it might be like to be that person in a space where there are people becoming and being allies. Envision being that person surrounded by people communicating their curiosities about LGBTQQ people and their histories, satisfying those curiosities by reading LGBTQ-themed texts, and engaging in provocative dialogue across differences, including, but not limited to, those defined by sexual and gender identities and expressions. Imagine the positive impact such a classroom and school could have on that person, those people, as well as others.

HAVING WHAT IT TAKES

It was my attempt to imagine what it would take to provide this kind of education that provoked me to ask the literature discussion group what it would be like to read these texts in their classes, and it is their answers that ground me. They talked about the significant roles of parents, specific texts, class communities, and particular students and teachers. What it would be like depended so much on all of these factors, they explained.

They reminded me of the fear of parents, both how teachers fear parental disapproval and how parents fear for their children, and how this fear resulted in the censorship of LGBTQ-themed texts. For example, in our first book discussion, Caroline asked whether parents would resist their reading and discussing LGBTQ-themed books in schools, and Jeff and Anna said simultaneously and unequivocally, "Yeah" and then,

> *Jeff*: Most definitely, parents would be all over that. They'd try to shut it down, or support it, whichever.
> *Caroline*: Without even reading the book?
> *Anna*: Yeah.
> *Caroline*: But, like you said it's just like any book about straight people.
> *Kim*: My dad says if it has a gay title, you're not reading it.

After the discussion we learned that Kim came to the meeting against her father's orders. Once he figured it out, he came to the youth center to get her. He was belligerent. I was afraid of him for Kim, her teacher who was also at the meeting, myself, and the group as a whole. Moreover, I was worried that we had put other people at the center at risk. Aside from his intimidating temper tantrum, his impact was minimal at the center, but the next day he met with Kim, her teacher, and their principal and, ultimately, withdrew Kim from the school to get her away from this "gay teacher" and her "gay books." Kim never returned to the school or the literature discussion group (Kenney, 2010).

Fear of parental disapproval among teachers and students is grounded and should not be thoughtlessly dismissed. But what was the source of Kim's father's anger? Kim's brother had come out as gay and, as a result, Kim's father kicked him out of their house and legally "emancipated" him. At this point, Kim was questioning her sexuality. I sincerely believe that Kim's father was afraid, also. He was afraid of homosexuality, and he was afraid of losing his daughter. In his mind, the two were connected. He believed that he lost his son to homosexuality, though I would argue that he pushed his son away with his homophobia and was in the process of doing the same thing with his daughter.

I wonder how Kim's father's relationships with his children might have been different if he had learned not to fear and hate homosexuality when he was in school. In order for this to be possible in schools, teachers must reflect on and directly address their fear of parental disapproval. We need to understand this disapproval as rooted in fear and hatred of that which is not normative in terms of sexuality and gender. In Butler's (1999) terms, these parents are trapped in the fiction of the "heterosexual matrix" in which men must be masculine, requiring attraction to women, and women must be feminine, requiring attraction to men.

Reading and discussing LGBTQ-themed literature offers one way to work within and against this matrix, but, as the youth pointed out, one must consider many factors when thinking about how to do this in school. When we talked about which texts might be most suitable for classroom use, across the years, I noticed a troubling pattern. It seemed that texts that they either had read in school ("Am I Blue?" by Bruce Coville [1994] and "A Letter to Harvey Milk" by Lesléa Newman [1988]) or could easily imagine reading in school focused entirely on White gay men. A book they read in the group but could imagine reading in school "Santaland Diaries" (Sedaris, 1997) not only focused on a White gay man but also deemphasized his gay-ness. This is not a critique of Sedaris; his stories are in many ways delightful, and many of them could easily provoke an interrogation of the heterosexual matrix. Texts that just focus on White gay men, however, leave little room for talking about intersecting identities, including but not limited to race, class, gender, and religion. And texts that fail to foreground queer themes limit opportunities for discussion of heteronormativity (Greenbaum, 1994; Sumara & Davis, 1999).

The class communities also determine whether LGBTQ-themed texts could be read, according to the youth. In our first book discussion, focused on *Boy Meets Boy*—which is also mostly about White gay males but which does, at least, confront homophobia and heterosexism directly—the youth considered what it might be like to read this book in class. In doing so they pointed to three kinds of classes. One was characterized as "a handful class" comprising mostly "all-American boys." It was hypothesized that these boys would not even read such a text unless it counted as a grade and then they would "give constant commentary," to quote a teacher. Anna said that these boys would not "bash [gay people] or anything . . . [but] they'd be so close-minded," and her teacher agreed. Another class they described would, according to Jeff, "adapt . . . really quickly" and "rock through this," according to his teacher. The third class they described was more complicated. Debbie asked Melissa, one of her students, about their shared class in particular.

Melissa: I don't think that, maybe a few people, because, you know Rebecca, she's in my English class?
Debbie: Yeah.
Melissa: Maybe only a few people in our English class would want to read it. The other people not so much I don't think. But that could be just because their parents just won't even let them, so they think, "I can't even read this book. I won't even go there."

Melissa pointed to Rebecca here because Rebecca, like Melissa, had a lesbian sister, who therefore, Melissa seemed to suggest, would want to read and discuss a LGBTQ-themed text in class. The next week, in fact, she explicitly stated, "*I* like to talk about it." She recognized, however, that others in the class might not want to, but she attributed that to their parents' homophobia rather than her peers' homophobia.

Implicit in all of this talk about the class, though, is that it depends on the students. That is, it would be better, or at least easier, to read and discuss LGBTQ-themed texts in classes that include people like Melissa and Rebecca and more difficult in classes that include the "all-American boys," who, in Jeff's words, would "refuse to read it" or "say something stupid." Anna summarized the range of student reactions to LGBTQ-themed texts, in this case *Boy Meets Boy*, by saying:

> I think that people who are not so close-minded and open would enjoy the book and find that the book's not just about gay people, and find it's more than that. And then, but, I still think that there will be people who would just hate it and hate them.

This wide range of classes and students seems to me exactly the reason to read and discuss LGBTQ-themed texts in school, to engage some students while challenging others. As Anna stated, it is imperative to challenge students:

> For someone who's like, like they disapprove of gay people, if like you get past it just being about gay people, like you find out it's an actual love story. Like it says right here, "Noah is right on time, he brought me flowers, I want to cry. I'm such a sop right now, I'm so happy." Like you could think that even if they are gay, like they can still have feelings and they still love people, and I just like that.

And later in the same discussion, she said, to fail to provide such challenging opportunities is "sad because [they] could learn so many . . . views of everything, and then maybe they could understand more." The youth reminded me, though, of the importance of the teacher.

Both Anna and Melissa said that what it would be like to read and discuss LGBTQ-themed texts in class "depends upon the teacher." Anna and Jeff talked about this in specific terms with their teacher Debbie:

> *Anna*: Like with you [referring to Debbie] I'd be fine, but if I had another English teacher or just another teacher, like if I had

like Mr. Matthews or something, I'm not sure I would be this comfortable . . .

Jeff: Our social studies teacher, I don't think I'd ever talk to him about this.

The variability of teachers' stances toward LGBTQQ people troubles the implication that LGBTQ-themed texts should, indisputably, be used in classes. Such texts cannot be used by all teachers well. For example, a teacher who has not yet reflected on his or her own homophobia might do more damage to LGBTQQ students by engaging this literature than by dismissing it entirely. Such a teacher might not have enough information about LGBTQQ people to answer questions students might ask. The teacher might use offensive terminology. He or she might unintentionally convey disgust when encountering LGBTQQ characters. This is precisely why ally teachers are needed. Take for example, a student teacher of Caroline's who was doing her internship with some of the young people in this literature discussion group. This student teacher and ally facilitated a discussion around the gay-themed short story, "Am I Blue?" (Coville, 1994). People reported that she "handled that class well" and that while "there were people who felt uncomfortable talking about it . . . no one was rude about it, real respectful, a lot of people got into it." The talk of the youth here suggests to me the importance of teachers in nurturing student allies.

PRACTITIONER APPLICATIONS: NURTURE STUDENT ALLIES

This chapter offers clear recommendations for teachers and youth service providers who strive to nurture student allies:

- Recognize your complicity in oppressing marginalized populations, whether by ignoring homophobia, hindering ally behavior, or otherwise.
- Assert an ally identity and work diligently to develop it.
- Believe that some of your students are be(com)ing allies; create contexts in which this is acceptable.
- Start a GSA; advertise the GSA; be explicit about the nature of the group.
- Select, read, recommend, and discuss a broad range of texts with students that both connect with their experiences as well as inform them of the experiences of people unlike them in significant ways.

- Use these texts to teach about the histories and presence of diverse populations, including but not limited to LGBTQQ people.
- In the discussion of such texts, point to things allies do. Include their successes and struggles.
- Name, too, the pleasures and challenges of marginalized people.
- In discussions of desires, attractions, and dating, be open to those not defined rigidly.
- Initiate and facilitate conversations across differences, including with parents and administrators.

Although I use allies much like GLSEN does, that is, in reference to people who advocate for LGBTQQ people, it helps here to think of allies more broadly as people who advocate on behalf of any marginalized populations (Clark, 2010). In this way, the above suggestions can be applied generously.

It is not enough for LGBTQQ youth to work against homophobia and heterosexism in schools, even as straight student allies join them. Both need the support of ally teachers. With this in mind, I turn, in the next chapter, to a teacher inquiry group committed to combating heterosexism and homophobia in classrooms and schools.

5

Be(com)ing Teacher Allies

As suggested in Chapter 4, teachers in general, and literacy teachers in particular, can play significant roles in supporting the anti-homophobia efforts of LGBTQQ and ally students. They can do so whether or not they are LGBTQQ, as long as they are also allies. Like the students discussed in the previous chapters, teachers must be committed not just to being allies but also always becoming allies. To illustrate what this means, I turn to what I have experienced as part of an inspirational teacher inquiry group called the Pink TIGers (Blackburn, Clark, Kenney, & Smith, 2010). The group began meeting in central Ohio in August 2004 and has been meeting monthly since. It has comprised teachers of elementary, middle, secondary, and post-secondary students, both LGBTQQ and ally and both novice and experienced, who have shared a commitment to combating homophobia in schools. I include myself among these teachers.

As teachers, we actively attended to how we identified and the consequences of our identifications. We deliberately educated ourselves on issues pertinent to LGBTQQ populations. We also put out homophobic fires, metaphorically speaking, and celebrated anti-homophobic accomplishments. We strove to create supportive contexts for our LGBTQQ and straight ally students through extracurricular efforts, curriculum and pedagogy, and policy work. Moreover, our efforts extended to district and even statewide policy making. Ultimately, as activist teachers, we educated other teachers in a variety of ways, which I discuss later in this chapter.

CHALLENGES AND RISKS OF SELF-IDENTIFICATION

To be(come) a teacher ally poses more distinct challenges for LGBTQQ teachers (Jackson, 2007; Mayo, 2001; Rofes, 1995) than for straight teachers.[1] One of the challenges for LGBTQQ teachers is whether to come out to their co-workers and/or students. Brian, for example, a White gay man found that just coming out to some of his co-workers improved the quality of his teaching life. Therefore, he was trying to come out, gradually, but he had not yet come out to the students in his district. Lauren and Maree, who also are White, talked passionately about how important it was to come out so that their students' homophobic stereotypes were challenged and so that students who identified as something-other-than-straight would understand that this was not something to be ashamed of.

Still, the teachers in this group recognized and experienced some of the risks associated with being out as a teacher, such as being falsely accused of trying to recruit students into being LGBTQQ. Lauren, for example, had two students who she knew had been removed from her charter high school because of parental concerns regarding her being an out lesbian (Kenney, 2010). Anette was troubled by a different sort of risk. She had been an elementary school teacher in an urban school where most of the teachers were White and most of the students were Black. As a biracial teacher (German and African American), Anette felt like it was more important for her to be a role model for her students as a person of color than as a gay woman. She worried that being the latter might negate the former, that is, her being gay may call into question whether she was a worthy role model as a person of color (Melvin, 2010). This was a risk she was unwilling to take.

Risks, though, were not limited to LGBTQQ teachers. For example, Jill, a White straight ally, took a leave of absence to pursue her doctorate. When she returned, the position she left as a high school English teacher at the school where she had been since its inception was open, but she was assigned to an English teaching position split between two middle schools. She felt certain that this assignment was punishment for her assertive and effective efforts at sponsoring a GSA, which her principal at the time did not support. Teachers who wish to engage in ally work (Clark, 2010) need to recognize, accept, and prepare themselves for risks and to understand that these risks vary from person to person.

Straight allies also experience anxiety around their self-identifications, much like LGBTQQ teachers do. Caroline, for example, wondered whether it was appropriate for her to identify herself as an ally or whether that was a title that should be bestowed upon her by an LGBTQQ person. Jill struggled less with identifying as an ally and more with being a straight ally sponsoring her school's GSA. She was concerned about whether she knew enough about issues pertinent to LGBTQQ people to provide adequate support for club members. Jill addressed this concern, as well as others, by educating herself.

EDUCATION THROUGH DISCUSSION, RESOURCES, AND INQUIRY

All of the Pink TIGers educated themselves independently and collectively. As we became increasingly aware of trans-phobia, for example, individuals listened to reports on National Public Radio (NPR) that explored the topic of transgender youth and watched films such as *Rent* and *Transamerica*. This resulted in a group discussion in which we compared the superficial representation of transpeople in *Rent* versus the complex one in *Transamerica*. We not only learned about a wide array of resources from one another, we also had chances to hear about one another's unique experiences, to encounter multiple perspectives on related current events, and to grapple together with dilemmas pertinent to LGBTQQ people in schools.

Listening to one another describe our unique experiences often proved to be educative, particularly across lines of difference. For example, a straight ally argued that people's homophobia can be convincingly combated by sharing a friendship with someone who turns out to be gay. She said,

> Like people can say, "No, no, no, [being gay is] awful, awful." And then I'm friends with you and I don't know you're gay and then three years from now, I find out, then I'm like, "Oh she's my friend and I already know her."

This assertion prompted reactions from two lesbians in the group, both of whom recalled times when they had lost friends by coming out to them. Through this interaction, a straight ally shifted the responsibility of combating homophobia from allies of LGBTQQ people, and, in response, two lesbians repositioned the responsibility as ultimately onto the homophobe. This pointed to the shared responsibility among straight allies, LGBTQQ people, and even homophobes to combat homophobia.

Current events were also central to the TIGers' educative discussions. For example the group talked about same-sex marriage laws around the country, debating the strengths and weaknesses of particular cases. The group also struggled with the roles educators played (and failed to play) in the junior high school where Lawrence King was shot to death by a classmate just after King came out as gay and conveyed his attraction for the perpetrator. The juxtaposition of Rick Warren, an evangelical Christian leader opposed to same-sex marriages, and Gene Robinson, the first out gay and non-celibate Episcopalian priest, as speakers at President Obama's inaugural events also prompted much discussion. By talking together about current events pertinent to LGBTQQ people, we were challenged both to support our stances and, at times, to change them.

The group also talked about particular situations that we were struggling with individually. For example, many of us struggled with the apparent conflict between being a religious person and an advocate for LGBTQQ people. We talked at great length about what the specific conflicts were and how people from different perspectives made sense of the conflicts differently. These discussions were enriched by the range of religious positions members brought to the group, from currently practicing within particular faiths to having made a conscious rejection of faith-based practices, as well as by the range of experiences members had had with religious people, from positive ally work to aggressive homophobia. Perhaps most compelling was when some of our stereotypes of religious people as homophobic people were disrupted. Ariel and Ryan, for example, worked in a district where there was a gay-straight-Christian alliance who advocated on behalf of their school's GSA by calling the school and offering their support, serving as a counter balance to the people who called expressing disgust and disappointment (Schey & Uppstrom, 2010). And it was from Maree's church's commitment to becoming a congregation that welcomes and affirms transgender people that our group came to know of, read, and discuss *Trans-Sister Radio* (Bohjalian, 2001). Without this range of perspectives, we might have maintained stereotypes against religious people and, thus, damaged relationships with significant allies or prevented them from developing. As these examples show, teachers discussing dilemmas among diverse people is one way for them to educate themselves.

There were other significant themes, though, in which we as a group lacked diversity. This was most obvious with regard to race. Most group members were White. Of regular participants, only Anette identified as biracial and Jenell as African American. This is not to say that the group did not benefit tremendously from the contributions of the people of color in the group. We did, unquestionably, but even so, most of us knew better than to expect one or two people to represent any racial group or to take on the burden of educating White people. Therefore, we actively sought educative resources, such as essays, films, and literature, to inform our understandings of, in this case, the intersectionality (Blackburn & McCready, 2009; Blackburn & Smith, 2010; Hancock, 2007; Kumashiro, 2001) of sexual, gendered, and racial identities. In struggling to understand intersectionality, we read Brant's (1991) collection of short stories that foreground gay and lesbian American Indian characters; Finnerty's (2004) letter to White LGBTQ people; hooks' (2000) essay on homophobia in Black communities; and Reeves' (1999) column about being Black, gay, and religious. We also watched *Brother to Brother* (Evans, 2004), which centers on a young Black gay man and his reflections on the Harlem Renaissance.

For all educators, in the scarcity or absence of any particular diversity, it is worthwhile to turn to alternative resources. This was imperative as the Pink TIGers strove to understand issues pertinent to transgender people, as no one in the group outwardly identified as such. There were, however, several group members who had committed themselves to advocating for transpeople. Jill and Lauren, for example, had screened *Ma Vie en Rose* with their GSAs and invited transgender guest speakers to talk with their students. These group members challenged the rest of the group to learn more about transpeople and thus led the group in fighting trans-phobia. The group collectively agreed to read and discuss *Trans-Sister Radio* (Bohjalian, 2001), and, because the novel is written by a straight ally, we agreed to pair it with an article by Ellen Wittlinger, a straight ally and author of young adult literature that incorporates lesbian, gay, bisexual, transgender, and questioning characters.[2] In the article, Wittlinger, who has been nominated for a Lambda Literary Award three times, responds to the foundation's recent commitment to award LGBT writers rather than straight ally authors.

Even with topics many of us knew quite a bit about, we sought resources for our continued learning. To learn more about LGBTQQ history, for example, we went to see *Milk* (Van Sant, 2008) and even just to understand what it was like to be gay in very different times and places, we went to see *Brokeback Mountain* (Lee, 2005). To learn more about engaging young people with topics related to lesbian and gay people, we watched *It's Elementary* (Cohen & Chasnoff, 1996) and the "Sugartime" episode of *Postcards from Buster* (Gunther, 2005) and read chapters from Spurlin's (2000) *Lesbian and Gay Studies and the Teaching of English*. This is, by no means, an exhaustive list and is not intended to be.[2] Rather, my point is to emphasize the importance of turning to a wide array of resources when educating one's self about what it means to be(come) a teacher ally.

A final and significant way that teachers can educate themselves as they strive to advocate for LGBTQQ people in their schools is through teacher inquiry projects. Many of the Pink TIGers conducted inquiry projects into their own classrooms, schools, and districts. Lauren, for example, explored the significance of her coming out as a lesbian in her secondary English classroom only to discover the "danger of a single story" (Adichie, 2009), that is, by only offering one image of what it means to be gay, she ostracizes students unlike her in other ways, such as gay men or lesbians of color. This inquiry propelled her into another in which she challenged herself to include a variety of queer-inclusive texts in her curriculum and reflected on the results of her efforts. Such on-going "systematic and intentional inquiry" (Cochran-Smith & Lytle, 1993) holds great promise in terms of teachers' self-education.

Teachers who actively struggle with their self-identifications and self-educations with respect to sexuality, gender, and related oppressions position themselves as allies who can advocate for LGBTQQ people in and beyond schools. It is such advocacy that I discuss next.

RECOGNIZING AND REACTING TO HOMOPHOBIA IN SCHOOLS

Teachers interested in becoming allies of LGBTQQ people are often surprised by how much homophobia they start seeing in their schools. They have noticed the most overt performances of homophobia, such as physical assaults, but they begin noticing more subtle homophobic performances—things to which they are so accustomed that they had hardly noticed them before, such as the use of the word gay as a negative generic descriptor or the use of the word fag to police masculine gender rules and regulations (Pascoe, 2007). When these teachers commit to attending to such forms of homophobia, they are inundated with their ubiquity of those forms. They are faced with the dilemma of whether to punish the people using such words in such ways or to educate those people and, if the latter, trying to find the time to do so when the words are used so frequently by so many people. Jason struggled with this issue, sometimes finding himself chiding students for their homophobic language and other times explaining the history of hate behind *fag*, for example. Jason was never fully satisfied with either approach but recognized the need for both in order to interrupt and educate (Gonzales, 2010).

In addition to navigating such ubiquitous performances of homophobia, educators must also respond to the more uniquely situated ones. For example, several teachers sponsored their schools' GSAs and created announcements and fliers advertising the clubs. Sometimes the students reading the announcements on the schoolwide sound system refused or were prohibited from saying the phrase *gay-straight alliance*; they would only say the acronym. This was problematic in that students who were not already familiar with the club would not likely recognize the acronym, so the club would only serve students who were already in-the-know. Teachers had to insist that their GSAs received the same treatment as other clubs, including but not limited to the FCA, or the Fellowship of Christian Athletes. Other times, posted GSA fliers were damaged or destroyed. Some teachers watched them dogmatically and punished people who they caught vandalizing them and asked their supportive colleagues to join them in their efforts. Other teachers kept a huge reserve of fliers and replaced them when necessary. One teacher put messages to vandals on the backs of signs, such as, "If you are reading this, you have an irrational fear of gay people."

Teacher allies, frustratingly, must also contend with the homophobia of their co-workers. Jill witnessed teachers engaging in homophobic teasing of one another. She watched one male teacher mock the male athletic director by posting his name on the women's restroom door. The joke seemed to Jill both misogynistic and homophobic; she confronted the teacher by asking how he would explain this joke should a student ask about it. In response, the man removed the sign.

Sometimes teachers' homophobia negatively impacts students (Kosciw et al., 2008). In Jenell's school, for example, all students who were identified as female in their school records and were scheduled to be recognized at either the school's National Honor Society (NHS) induction or graduation were required by a single teacher who sponsored these events to wear skirts or dresses. This rule was applied even to students who had earned the recognitions but self-identified in ways that were in conflict with their assigned gender of girl. One student who had a 3.7 GPA was not inducted to the NHS because she refused to wear a dress; another student was forbidden from participating in the NHS induction because, in the sponsor's words, "She walk[ed] like a man."

Jenell talked with the principal who agreed that the sponsor's rules were problematic and to talk with the affected students. Her motivation, though, was more likely a student's recent threat to contact local media about related issues than it was Jenell's concern. This suspicion is supported by the fact that the principal also told Jenell that students should communicate their concerns to the principal directly, hinting at her desire to avoid media attention. As it turns out, the student did not contact the media, and the principal did not contact the students. Alternatively, Jenell talked with the sponsor directly. Jenell described the conversation as generally cooperative but ineffective. She had suggested as an alternative rule that "girls be permitted to wear crop pants, gauchos, or if they identified as male, be permitted to wear the dress pants and dress shirts," which the sponsor understood as something more like "OK, if they are female, wear the dress. If they want to be male, wear the pants." Ultimately, Jenell told the students in her GSA to "wear the white pants suits or the gauchos to graduation if they wanted to. They did and it went smoothly."

As Jenell's account reveals, teacher allies are, thankfully, not limited to interrupting and educating. They also get opportunities to celebrate the successes of anti-homophobic efforts. Jill, for example, watched one of her students claim space in her classroom by clearing off a bookshelf for GSA materials and labeling it as such, and Lauren saw a student rebut a teacher's homophobic statement. Jason witnessed one of his effeminate male students present, as his culminating project around the class's reading of *Romeo and Juliet*, a queer version of the Capulet ball, in which both opposite- and same-sex couples flirted and courted. In fact, all of the teachers in this group noticed an increased level of comfort among LGBTQQ students and their allies in their schools over the years. Although this may be understood as representative of a positive cultural shift in society more broadly, I do not think it is. If such a shift were responsible, I would hear such accounts from the wide array of teachers with whom I work beyond this project. Rather their observations are related to the very important anti-homophobia work these teachers do in their classrooms and schools.

GAY-STRAIGHT ALLIANCES

It is teacher allies that students approach when they want to start a GSA. Teacher allies who know the history and present legal context for sponsoring GSAs are better equipped to support students in this effort. (The documentary *Out of the Past* (Dupre, 1998) is one resource that may be of use in this regard.) GSAs that are initiated by students but sponsored by teacher allies are most likely to garner support. If administrative support is denied, the GSA can still be pursued, particularly if there are any other clubs in the school. Following the general guidelines for school clubs, even if these guidelines are more rigorous than what is typically practiced, is advisable. Otherwise, efforts to start a GSA may be met with resistance or even rejection that may seem to some legitimate. (For a more developed description and discussion of how to start a GSA, see MacGillivray's 2007 handbook on the topic.) Many of the Pink TIGers started GSAs at their schools and experienced such resistance and rejection in a variety of forms. Dana, for example, was advised by her principal to start a Diversity Club instead of a GSA. Although she tried this, she found that in an effort to include a wide range of diversity, the focus on LGBTQQ people was diluted almost to the point of disappearing. Eventually, though, she was able to start and facilitate an active GSA.

Pink TIGers who sponsored GSAs, whether or not they initiated them, struggled with their roles and expectations. Since most of the GSA sponsors in the group were straight allies, they toiled over how to serve LGBTQQ students the best, recognizing that they themselves had a limited understanding of the experiences of coming out as something-other-than-straight. They relied on films and guest speakers—and in Jill's case, even guest sponsors—to complement their knowledge of what some of their students might be enduring.

Just as the sponsors struggled with their roles, they grappled with students' roles or with their expectations of students. The common tension was around the social-versus-activist nature of the groups. At one meeting Jill described the conflict in this way, saying,

> One of my concerns is that in GSA work at schools, that it's not, I don't know, but I wonder if it's being done in a way that's really troubling the system or if it's just being put into place in a way that's just making it popular. Like I think all the kids that were at [an event the Pink TIGers hosted to end that year's Day of Silence and to begin

a literature discussion group] were really great, but I don't know if they're really going into the deeper parts of the issues. I'm not saying that you have to do that every time with kids who are 15 or 16, but the popularity of it and just everyone kind of jumping. I don't want the kids to just be following me or following anything without troubling it, looking at it, you know. It's not, I don't know. . . . Well do you have to trouble everything or can you just jump in and have a good time with it and not be so serious?

Underlying Jill's observations, critiques, and questions are her activist values. In other words, she, like others in the group, want their GSAs to be activist-oriented. Later in the same meeting, Jill wondered how her GSA could possibly be activist when it was so isolated. She said,

One of the really hard things about the GSA is you're always preaching to the choir even when you do get into like prompting them to ask questions. At least that has been my experience in my instance. Like we're having this conversation in my closed room.

It seemed to me, however, that maybe a balance was needed. In response to Jill, I said,

Sometimes I think of that as practice for the steps that are outside of that. . . . And it's like all that work that is behind closed doors or amongst choir or whatever, it's all just like getting strong enough to go to the prom together.

In other words, I wondered if young people needed to socialize in the safer context of the GSA so that they could prepare themselves to do what for them in their context was quite activist: attend the prom as a same-sex couple. Teacher allies who sponsor GSAs must both value the social work it accomplishes for students and challenge them to also engage in activist work that will make their schools better places for LGBTQQ people and their allies.

A local activist effort by some of the Pink TIGers' GSA students involved confronting teachers for actions the students understood to be homophobic. For example, a colleague of Jill's was teaching *Montana 1948* to a multicultural literature class that included several GSA students. In her teaching, the colleague compared being gay to having a disease and talked about how awful she would feel if any of her children identified as gay. Together, Jill's GSA crafted a letter to the teacher, which although it offended the teacher, resulted in a discussion in which Jill had the opportunity to offer suggestions for how the teacher might respond more generally and make it clear that she supports LGBTQQ students, which she stated she did.

Another way Pink TIGers' GSA students engaged in activist work was hosting a local event celebrating the National Day of Silence. "On the National Day of Silence hundreds of thousands of students nationwide take a vow of silence to bring attention to anti-LGBT name-calling, bullying and harassment in their schools" (http://www.dayofsilence.org/index.cfm). Students informed teachers of the event and their intended participation in advance, gave them written reminders on the day of the event, and wore small signs explaining their silence to others. There were some complaints from parents and teachers, and in Ariel and Ryan's school some students were even kept home from school in protest of the event. But overall the experience was positive and the effort successful. Jill even created and shared a slideshow of the Day of Silence event at her school.

As powerful as GSAs can be for some students, it is imperative to recognize their limits. Some teachers notice that their GSAs are populated mostly by straight girls who are actively claiming a more liberal identity. Others notice that their GSAs serve White LGBTQQ youth but not LGBTQQ youth of color. These patterns are not unique to our group or region, but are reflected nationwide (e.g., McCready, 2004b). For this reason, among others, it is important for teacher allies to engage in policy work as well.

CURRICULUM AND PEDAGOGY

Teacher allies also improve school climate for LGBTQQ students through their pedagogy and curriculum. Initially, teachers in the inquiry group thought it was best to let students select texts with LGBTQ-themes or choose to present on topics pertinent to LGBTQQ people. This approach would dissuade administrative and parental critique and, thus, seem to dodge their censorship.

Youth, however, pointed out the problems with this approach. Young people in the literature discussion group talked about how when a student chooses to read a book with LGBTQ-themes, the student is assumed to be LGBTQQ and therefore becomes vulnerable to his or her peers' homophobia. This dynamic pushes students to self-censor. When a teacher assigns an LGBTQ-themed text, though, the student evades the assumption and the related abuse. Dara, from The Attic, also described how if a student chooses to present from an ally perspective, then the student is similarly vulnerable to peers' homophobia. But, a student may safely choose an opposing perspective, exposing everyone in the class to that student's homophobia. Recall the story in Chapter 3, when Dara's classmates selected and presented their opinions, rather than research, on the topic of gay people in the military. Their position, as Dara heard it, was that they believed gay people should not be in the military because they could not be trusted not to have sex in the residential quarters. This reveals the homophobic assumption that gay people are hypersexual and thus unwilling to control their sexual drive, or, worse still, that they are likely to force sex upon unwilling partners, that is, rape straight people. Moreover, Dara felt the classmates directed their presentation directly at her. It is not surprising, then, that students self-censor when it comes to selecting LGBTQ-themed texts in schools. While student-choice is supported generally as a strategy for literacy classrooms (Daniels, 2002), for LGBTQ-themed texts, the role of a teacher as initiator and facilitator takes on new importance in creating a safer space for all students.

Ultimately, much of the Pink TIGers' discussions revolved around what texts and topics they could bring into their curriculum and how they could engage students in issues pertinent to LGBTQQ people. They have accomplished these goals in both subtle and overt ways. Jason talked about challenging his students' heterosexist assumptions by asking his students to consider whether there could be romantic or sexual tension between Romeo and Mercutio. Maree, on the other hand, brought an image of Carl Joseph Walker-Hoover to her 12-student reading group in a high poverty public school. She asked these 4th graders to write about their impressions of Walker-Hoover based on the photo, which pictured an African American 11-year-old boy smiling, holding a football, and wearing a black and gold football jersey and shoulder pads. She asked them whether they would want to be friends with him. Students initially responded very positively about the boy in the photograph until Maree told them that just that month this 6th-grade boy hung himself after regularly enduring homophobic bullying, even though he did not self-identify as gay. Maree then facilitated a discussion about homophobic bullying in their school, challenging students to acknowledge the potential consequences of such abuse. Thus, Jason challenged heterosexism discreetly, and Maree challenged homophobia head on.

According to the Pink TIGers, their curricular and pedagogical efforts made a difference in combating homophobia in classrooms. Jill talked about how her classroom discussion of *The Women of Brewster Place* (Naylor, 1982) conveyed some of her students' developing understandings of lesbian hate crimes. Lauren surveyed her students before and after using a collection of texts with queer themes in her curriculum and found that they expressed less discomfort with issues related to LGBTQQ people over time (Kenney, 2010). Teachers who manage to overcome the censorship of LGBTQ-themed texts are well-positioned to engage in the challenging work of be(com)ing allies themselves as well as challenging their students to do the same.

As important as curricular inclusion is, the significance of a provocative pedagogical approach cannot be underestimated. For the Pink TIGers, this meant negotiating threat lovingly. As described in Chapter 1, youth perceived to be LGBTQQ experience the threat of homophobia and hetero-sexism regularly in schools. As described in Chapter 4 and here in Chapter 5, even straight allies, both students and teachers, experience this sort of threat in schools. What we did not initially understand, but came to, was that in our efforts to combat homophobia and heterosexism in classrooms and schools, we also threatened others. We threatened the people around us, students and teachers, who fervently believed in the wrongness or sin-fulness of people who experience same-sex desire and/or fail to adhere to gender norms. We threatened even the people who implicitly assumed that although homosexuality isn't wrong or bad it is not as good as het-erosexuality, which is "normal." We threatened their values, their deeply held beliefs. We learned that threat is not unidirectional and wondered whether it was not, perhaps, universally bad or good. Fecho (2001) argues that threat is always present in classrooms, can be exasperated by a criti-cal approach but can be worked through via inquiry. According to Fecho, threat needs to be negotiated rather than eliminated.

Negotiating tension, though, is complicated. Teacher allies want to combat homophobia in an effort to create allies. We want to push hard on peoples' homophobic and heterosexist values—but not so hard that the people dismiss us, turn away, stop listening. It is a fine line, and every-one's line is drawn at a different place, which may change from day-to-day, even moment-to-moment.

Allen (2007) acknowledges the challenge and looks to Freire (1970) to find her way through the tiny space between "impossible" and "all but impossible." According to Allen, navigating this space requires that we re-main in dialogue, not just in conversation, but in interactions among peo-ple coming to understand one another's perspectives by naming them. Such dialogue can be, and I think Fecho would argue, will be threatening. Negotiating such threat demands a love of the world and for the people in it, a humility that allows you to believe in others' knowledge, a faith in humankind, an active hope that the world will become a better place, and active thinking about how to make it so (pp. 87–88).

POLICY AND POLITICS

Policy work on behalf of LGBTQQ people might include advocating for partner benefits in communities where same-sex unions are not legally sanctioned, anti-discrimination policies that include sexual orientation and gender expression, curricular efforts to include LGBTQQ populations, and anti-bullying policies. These are just some of the approaches used by the Pink TIGers. I focus here on our collective and individual efforts to get enumerated language in state-, district-, and schoolwide anti-bullying policies to protect LGBTQQ people.

In December 2006, the Ohio state legislators allowed testimonies pertinent to House Bill 276, Schools—Anti-bullying Policies. The bill was an important one but failed to name protected populations and, therefore, left it up to administrators, who, like everyone, have their own sets of biases and prejudices that determined who would and who would not be protected. Provoked by Angie, the then-executive director of the local center for LGBTQ youth, three of the Pink TIGers, including myself, testified; a fourth Pink TIGer brought three of her students to testify. Our testimonies were among those offered by leaders of Ohio LGBTQ organizations, a law professor, and a parent of a gay son whose life ended in suicide.

The one person who argued against enumerated language was the Ohio School Boards Association lobbyist, who claimed that, "harassment in one school may not be harassment in another" and "there is too much liability for schools if the categories are enumerated." I shared Angie's interpretation of this speaker's message, which was "Some populations will be safe in some schools, but not in others. Some kids will be safe, and others won't. It will depend on where you go to school. We can't afford to do better than this." An amendment with enumerated language was proposed and declined. The bill devoid of enumerated language was passed.

The following summer, however, the General Assembly created a model policy intended to help districts shape their anti-bullying policies. The model initially included enumerated language including sexual orientation but not gender expression. When the model was brought to the State Board of Education for approval, though, the enumerated language was debated and deleted because it made some school officials "uncomfortable."

The state then required districts to create their own anti-bullying policies based on the bill and the "model." Pink TIGers, including Jill, worked to get on these districtwide committees. The schools in Jill's district already had schoolwide anti-bullying policies with enumerated language that included sexual orientation and gender expression, but rather than adapting these existing policies, the district dropped them in favor of the state's evasive model. Jill worked with her colleagues to undo this damage by asserting themselves on the already established committee. They were repeatedly avoided and aggressively ignored, so, they shifted their efforts from the districtwide committee to schoolwide committees. In this way, they managed to get the anti-bullying policy with enumerated language approved, "nearly unanimously," at two of the three high schools in the district. The school-based policies, however, were entirely disregarded. As Jill said, "We went the route they sent us on and guess what? It was a goose chase."

Jill's next attempt was to talk directly with the district's superintendent. She shared documentation of her colleagues' efforts and her own, and he agreed that they had been "deliberately lead down the wrong paths." He stated that he would take care of the enumerated language because it was the "right thing to do and it would be immoral not to do it." He claimed that it would be done in June of that year, and it was. It seemed that "having a friend in a 'big' position is the best way to get things done. The man cut through 7 months of intensive work with what would amount to a stroke of his pen. So, I wonder what would've happened if he hadn't been supportive. What would've worked then?" But I am not sure that "the man" would have made this particular "stroke of his pen" had Jill not been able to point to her "intensive work." (For a more developed description and discussion of a single district engaging in LGBT-inclusive policy work, see MacGillivray's *Sexual Orientation and School Policy* [2004].)

I think Jill's policy work, like that of other Pink TIGers, was often tedious and sometimes degrading but was also imperative. Even if the superintendent had not come along to save the day, Jill's laudable efforts resulted in developing community among ally teachers and educating others about the lives of LGBTQQ youth in their schools and district.

EDUCATING OTHERS

Just as teacher allies must educate themselves, they must also educate others. The Pink TIGers accomplished this both locally and nationally. Collectively, the Pink TIGers worked in collaboration with various invested groups within a local university—the local queer youth center, the local queer center, the local trans-advocacy center, an alternative school—and the producer of *It's Elementary* and *It's Still Elementary* to screen these films and facilitate panel discussions for pre-service teachers, in-service teachers, and parents. Moreover, the Pink TIGers spent NCTE grant funding on resources for teachers striving to become teacher allies and included a teacher's guide associated with the films *And Tango Makes Three*, for elementary teachers, and *Am I Blue?* for middle and high school teachers.

The Pink TIGers regularly presented at national conferences, reaching teacher audiences at the annual conferences of the National Council of Teachers of English (NCTE), teacher researcher audiences at the practitioner inquiry day of the Ethnography in Education Research Forum, and educational researcher audiences at the annual meetings of the American Educational Research Association (AERA). Many of these presentations developed into chapters in the Pink TIGers' edited book (Blackburn et al., 2010). In other words, the more this group of teacher allies learned about the obstacles to combating homophobia in schools and how to overcome those obstacles, the more seriously they took their responsibility to educate others.

ALLIES AMONG ALLIES

Just because the Pink TIGers were willing and able to educate others both locally and nationally does not mean we were ever done educating ourselves. This past year, for example, the group decided to select, read, and discuss books for meetings. Furthermore, the group has committed to yet another year of meeting—its eighth year, and this year they've decided to design an educative year-long project. Across our years of meeting together, I have come to believe that teacher allies are much more likely to continue to become allies among people who negotiate threat lovingly. The pedagogy for which I advocate earlier in this chapter must be adapted for those be(com)ing teacher allies.

I learned this most clearly with my colleague and friend, Jeane. Our collegial relationship really developed when we worked together to found the Pink TIGers, but our friendship progressed significantly when we figured out how to negotiate threat lovingly across our differences. In the early years of the Pink TIGers, I had two interactions with Jeane that offended me and stuck with me. I describe them here not to indict Jeane—as I said, we've become quite good friends—but to illustrate the dangerous possible outcomes when colleagues fail to negotiate lovingly, effectively indicting myself more than Jeane.

The first of the two incidents was during the fall of 2004. It was when Ohioans and others around the country were voting on whether same-sex couples should have the right to marry. In Ohio, it was already illegal for people of the same-sex to marry, but this was apparently not enough, because the people of the state elected to amend the state's constitution to limit marriage to being between one man and one woman. Within this political context, Jeane missed a Pink TIGer meeting to get married. I couldn't believe that an ally would actively engage in an institution that has always been implicitly heterosexist but at this moment in time was audaciously heterosexist. My feelings were hurt, and I was angry, but I said nothing to Jeane.

The second interaction was just over a year later when Jeane told a fascinating story about how it was not until long after she was married and in graduate school that she witnessed a romantic, committed relationship that she described as "harmonious," and this relationship was between two women. She then said, "I was really lucky to happen upon [my current husband] because I was beginning to think you could only get that kind of gentleness, reciprocal love, equality in a relationship with another woman." What I heard, though, was Jeane saying she felt lucky not to be a lesbian, which I translated into her feeling lucky to be not like me. I could only understand her comment as homophobic. Again, I was hurt and angry, and again, I said nothing to Jeane.

My hurt, anger, and silence became explosive much later in the same year when Jeane exposed her vulnerability as an ally. She described how she prepared her students for work around issues pertaining to sexual identities by using inclusive language, naming homophobia in the context of discussing oppression and including scholarly articles about how homophobia and heterosexism impact work in schools. The student, who was not only a practicing teacher but also a teacher with whom Jeane's program placed student teachers, refused to read or respond to these articles because doing so was against the student's religion. When Jeane asked for a justification, the student said, "Nothing that deals with this issue is valid in my point of view." Further the student said, "That is not what I do in my job. And if someone told me I had to, I would quit teaching in a public school." Jeane explained that her administrators directed her to go to legal affairs, where she was advised to give the student an incomplete and require the student to select and interpret scholarship related to "issues of gender and sexuality in schools." Not surprisingly, the student completed the assignment using readings that conveyed objections to LGBTQ-inclusive content in schools and thus passed the class and continued in the program. I was furious. I fumed, "That's crap. That's crap." My hurt, anger, and earlier silence prevented me from empathizing with Jeane's vulnerability and recognizing her efforts at combating heterosexism and homophobia in schools.

I'm left wondering what might have happened if I had negotiated threat lovingly. What if I had initially struggled to find words about how hurt I was when Jeane got married and thus given her a chance to tell me what marriage meant to her at the time? What if I had challenged what I understood to be Jeane's comment about being lucky not to be a lesbian and thus provided her with an opportunity to clarify her intention?

Years later, though, Jeane and I talked about the tensions between us. The first discussion was a difficult one. I was humbled by her willingness to talk with me one-on-one and embarrassed by my antagonistic behavior. She modeled for me what it meant to negotiate threat lovingly. She told me about her experiences in non-accusatory ways and thus invited me to do the same. This conversation led me to reinterpret her as an ally and to understand allies as always becoming. Whether my early interpretation of Jeane as heterosexist and homophobic was right or wrong is less important than my later interpretation of her as an ally. Heterosexism, homophobia, and "allyism" are not mutually exclusive, not just for Jeane, not just for straight allies, but for all of us raised in communities that teach heterosexist and homophobic values, even if only implicitly. We cannot prevent people from learning these values, but we can work against them, in ourselves and in others. Teacher allies are committed to working against hateful values but not absolved of them. The hope lies in the always be(com)ing allies among allies, that is, working among diverse people with shared commitments.

PRACTITIONER APPLICATIONS: BE(COME) AN ALLY

We need to understand ourselves and one another as be(com)ing allies in homophobic and heterosexist contexts, therefore embodying these values, while simultaneously fighting them. In this venture, I suggest the following:

- Brace yourself. There are risks involved.
- Never forget your privilege.
- Keep reading, watching, talking, listening, thinking, and feeling.
- Provide students with opportunities to do the same.
- Choose not to censor topics that acknowledge diversity in sexual orientations and gender expressions.
- Remember that just as there are some people who are uncomfortable engaging with topics pertinent to LGBTQQ people, there are others who are uncomfortable not doing so.
- Celebrate the successes of the community, including your own.
- Forgive yourselves and one another for embodying hateful values, love yourselves and one another for fighting them, and challenge yourselves and one another to keep up the fight.
- Be open to connecting with allies where you least expect them.

Even among allies, the fight can be threatening, and in the absence of love, threat can thwart or even abort our efforts. We can, indeed, we *must*, negotiate such threat lovingly.

Epilogue

Reading and writing words and worlds as an LGBTQQ student or teacher, or even on behalf of LGBTQQ students and teachers, is challenging work, no doubt. But the efforts of the LGBTQQ and ally students and teachers I describe here have had emancipatory results. They have changed lives—their own as well as others'.

Justine, for example, has graduated from college, works in a social service organization educating others about how to avoid contracting HIV/AIDS, and is grappling with what it means to be in a committed monogamous relationship. She has made a satisfying life for herself. Kira has also graduated from college. She currently works as a chef, and she and her partner of more than 10 years are trying to have children of their own. In a recent phone call she shared with me a conversation she had with her mom in which her mom expressed that her biggest regret was having pushed Kira out of her home when she came out as lesbian. Kira has made a positive life for herself, and in doing so, made an ally out of her mother.

Jill and her GSA just sponsored a Day of Silence event at her school, and there were many participants and no protesters, making evident how much her school has evolved with respect to being an inviting place for LGBTQQ people. Maree now teaches in a school in which she is out to everyone as a lesbian, which is imperative since it is the school her children attend. She is currently reading *Totally Joe* (Howe, 2005), a book about a middle school student coming to terms with being gay, with her 4th-grade students. Moreover, she is working with a researcher to document and study her efforts. She is actively making allies of and for the children in her classroom and in the school she shares with the children in her family.

I could go on and on with the amazing accomplishments of LGBTQQ and ally students and teachers through their reading and writing of words and worlds. All of the stories would reveal how complicated and inundating the work can be, but so too would they convey its value in that it makes the world a better place to live for ourselves, our children, and others, many, many others. In short, it's worth it.

Notes

Chapter 2

1. Many of the large schools in the district were, as a result of an earlier reform effort, divided into what were called small learning communities.

2. According to the Intersex Society of North America, "Intersex is a socially constructed category that reflects real biological variation" (http://www.isna.org/faq/what_is_intersex, ¶4). It references a "variety of conditions in which a person is born with a reproductive or sexual anatomy that doesn't seem to fit the typical definitions of female or male" (http://www.isna.org/faq/what_is_intersex, ¶1). For more information about intersex conditions, see http://www.isna.org/.

Chapter 3

1. It is not that they assumed that everyone was straight, rather, that heterosexism and homophobia made it acceptable to refer to people as if they were straight and unacceptable to imply some were not. The Speakers' Bureau members knew that some people in the audience were likely LGBTQQ, but they also knew that to have said that would have been perceived as a threat and put the audience on the defensive.

Part III

1. Although GLSEN's examples seem to imply a hierarchy of marginalization in which only one less marginalized than another can be an ally for that other. It seems to me, though, that marginalization as a hierarchy simply fails as does the suggested relationship between degrees of marginalization and ally work.

Chapter 5

1. These challenges are also different for lesbians, gay men, bisexual women, bisexual men, transgender individuals, and queer people, but this group focused on differences between lesbians and gay men, clustered together, and straight men and women, again, clustered.

2. For a fuller and annotated list of resources used by the Pink TIGers, see the annotated bibliography in *Acting Out!* (Blackburn, Clark, Kenney, & Smith, 2010).

References

Aarons, L. (1995). *Prayers for Bobby: A mother coming to terms with the suicide of her gay son*. New York: HarperOne.

Adichie, C. (2009). *The danger of a single story*. Retrieved from http://tedxproject.wordpress.com/2010/05/05/chimamanda-adichie-the-danger-of-a-single-story-3/

Allen, J. (2007). "So . . ." In M. V. Blackburn & C. T. Clark (Eds.), *Literacy research for political action and social change* (pp. 77–94). New York: Peter Lang.

Anzaldúa, G. (1987). *Borderlands/La fronteras: The new mestiza*. San Francisco, CA: Spinsters/Aunt Lute.

Athanases, S. Z. (1996). A gay-themed lesson in an ethnic literature curriculum: Tenth graders' responses to "Dear Anita." *Harvard Educational Review, 66*(2), 231–256.

Babcock, J. (2002). *The tragedy of Miss Geneva Flowers*. New York: Carroll & Graf.

Bass, E. (1993). For Barbara, who said she couldn't visualize two women together. In F. Howe (Ed.), *No more masks! An anthology of twentieth century American women poets* (pp. 408–409). New York: HarperPerennial.

Bechdel, A. (2006). *Fun home: A family tragicomic*. New York: Houghton Mifflin.

Blackburn, M. V. (2002/2003). Disrupting the (hetero)normative: Exploring literacy performances and identity work with queer youth. *Journal of Adolescent & Adult Literacy, 46*(4), 312–324.

Blackburn, M. V. (2003a). Exploring literacy performances and power dynamics at The Loft: Queer youth reading the world and word. *Research in the Teaching of English, 37*(4), 467–490.

Blackburn, M. V. (2003b). Losing, finding, and making space for activism through literacy performances and identity work. *Penn GSE Perspectives on Urban Education, 2*(1). Retrieved from http://www.urbanedjournal.org/articles/article0008.html

Blackburn, M. V. (2004). Understanding agency beyond school-sanctioned activities. In M. V. Blackburn & R. Donelson (Eds.), Sexual identities and schooling [Special issue]. *Theory into Practice, 43*(2), 102–110.

Blackburn, M. V. (2005). Talking together for change: Examining positioning between teachers and queer youth. In J. A. Vadeboncoeur & L. P. Stevens (Eds.), *Re/constructing "the adolescent": Sign, symbol and body* (pp. 249–270). New York: Peter Lang.

Blackburn, M. V. (2007). Gender rules and regulations as experienced and negotiated by queer youth. *Journal of Gay and Lesbian Issues in Education, 4*(2), 33–54.

Blackburn, M. V. (2008). Literacy performances of a gay young man in a book discussion group. In M. Harrison & M. J. Lingle-Martin (Eds.), *English Association of Pennsylvania schools and universities, 2007 Conference Proceedings*. Retrieved from http://eapsu.org/index.php?option=com_content&task=view&id=31

Blackburn, M. V., & Buckley, J. F. (2005). Teaching queer-inclusive English language arts. *Journal of Adolescent and Adult Literacy, 49*(3), 202–212.

Blackburn, M. V., & Clark, C. T. (2011). Becoming readers of literature with LGBT themes in and out of classrooms. In S. Wolf, K. Coats, P. Enciso, & C. Jenkins (Eds.), *Handbook of research on children's and young adult literature* (pp. 148–163). New York: Routledge.

Blackburn, M. V., Clark, C. T., Kenney, L. M., & Smith, J. M. (Eds.). (2010). *Acting out!: Combating homophobia through teacher activism*. New York: Teachers College Press.

Blackburn, M. V., & McCready, L. T. (2009). Voices of queer youth in urban schools: Possibilities and limitations. *Theory into Practice, 48*(3), 222–230.

Blackburn, M. V., & Smith, J. M. (2010). Moving beyond the inclusion of LGBT-themed literature in English language arts classrooms: Interrogating heteronormativity and exploring intersectionality. *Journal of Adolescent & Adult Literacy, 53*(8), 625–634.

Blount, J. M. (2006). *Fit to teach: Same-sex desire, gender, and school work in the twentieth century*. New York: State University of New York Press.

Board of Education, School District of Philadelphia. (1994). Policy 102. Retrieved from http://www.phila.k12.pa.us/offices/administration/policies/102.html

Bohjalian, C. (2001). *Trans-sister radio*. New York: Vintage.

Brant, B. (1991). *Food and spirits*. Ithaca, NY: Firebrand Books.

Britzman, D. P. (1997). What is this thing called love? New discourses for understanding gay and lesbian youth. In S. de Castell & M. Bryson (Eds.), *Radical in<ter>ventions: Identity, politics, and difference/s on educational praxis* (pp. 183–207). Albany: State University of New York Press.

Brown, R. M. (1988). *In her day*. New York: Bantam Books.

Brown, R. M. (2000). *Loose lips*. New York: Bantam Doubleday.

Burford, M. (2010). *The surge in gay teen suicide*. Retrieved from http://www.aol-health.com/2010/10/12/gay-teen-suicide-surge/

Butler, J. (1991). Imitation and gender insubordination. In D. Fuss (Ed.), *Inside/out: Lesbian theories, gay theories* (pp. 13–31). London, United Kingdom: Routledge.

Butler, J. (1999). *Gender trouble: Feminism and the subversion of identity* (2nd ed.). New York, NY: Routledge.

Calefati, J. (2008). Milwaukee to form gay-friendly middle school. *U.S. News On Education*. Retrieved from http://www.usnews.com/blogs/on-education/2008/12/17/milwaukee-to-form-gay-friendly-middle-school.html

Califia, P. (1996). *Doc and Fluff: The Dystopian tale of a girl and her biker*. Los Angeles: Alyson Books.

Carey-Webb, A. (2001). *Literature and lives: A response-based, cultural studies approach to teaching English*. Urbana, IL: NCTE.

Chbosky, S. (1999). *The perks of being a wallflower*. New York: MTV Books & Pocket Books.

Clark, C. T. (2010). Preparing LGBTQ-allies and combating homophobia in a U.S. teacher education program. *Teaching and Teacher Education, 26*(3), 704–713.

Clark, C. T., & Blackburn, M. V. (2009). Reading LGBT-themed literature with young people in classrooms: What's possible? *English Journal, 98*(4), 25–32.

Cochran-Smith, M., & Lytle, S. L. (1993). *Inside/outside: Teacher research and knowledge.* New York: Teachers College Press.

Cohen, H. S. (Producer) & Chasnoff, D. (Producer, Director). (1996). *It's elementary: Talking about gay issues in school* [Film/guide]. San Francisco: Women's Educational Media.

Consolacion, T. (2001). Where I am today. In K. Kumashiro (Ed.), *Troubling intersections of race and sexuality: Queer students of color and anti-oppressive education* (pp. 83–85). Lanham, MA: Rowman and Littlefield.

Coville, B. (1994). Am I blue? In M. D. Bauer (Ed.), *Am I blue? Coming out from the silence* (pp. 1–16). New York: HarperTrophy.

Daniels, H. (2002). *Literature circles: Voice and choice in book clubs and reading groups* (2nd ed.). Portland, ME: Stenhouse.

Davies, B., & Harré, R. (2001). Positioning: The discursive production of selves. In M. Wetherell, S. Taylor, & S. J. Yates (Eds.), *Discourse theory and practice* (pp. 264–271). Thousand Oaks, CA: Sage.

de Castell, S., & Jenson, J. (2007). No place like home: Sexuality, community, and identity among street-involved queer and questioning youth. In M. V. Blackburn & C. T. Clark (Eds.), *Literacy research for political action and social change* (pp. 131–152). New York: Peter Lang.

de Certeau, M. (1984). *The practice of everyday life.* Berkeley: University of California Press.

DeGeneres, E. (Producer), Anderson, J. (Director), & Coolidge, M. (Director). (2000). *If these walls could talk 2.* [TV]. HBO Home Video.

Driver, S. (2007). *Queer girls and popular culture: Reading, resisting, and creating media.* New York: Peter Lang.

Dupre, J. (Director). (1998). *Out of the past.* [Motion picture]. United States: Unipix.

Eidman-Aadahl, E. (2002). Got some time, got a place, got the word: Collaborating for literacy learning and youth development. In G. Hull & K. Schultz (Eds.), *School's out! Literacy at home, at work, and in the community.* New York: Teachers College Press.

Epstein, D. (2000). Reading gender, reading sexualities: Children and the negotiation of meaning in "alternative" texts. In W. J. Spurlin (Ed.), *Lesbian and gay studies and the teaching of English: Positions, pedagogies, and cultural politics* (pp. 213–233). Urbana, IL: National Council of Teachers of English.

Evans, R. (Director, Author). (2004). *Brother to brother* [Film]. Available from www.wolfevideo.com

Faderman, L. (1991). *Odd girls and twilight lovers: A history of lesbian life in twentieth century America.* New York: Columbia University Press.

Fecho, B. (2001). "Why are you doing this?": Acknowledging and transcending threat in a critical inquiry classroom. *Research in the Teaching of English, 36*(1), 9–37.

Finnerty, D. (2004). An open letter to my white lesbian, gay, bisexual, transgender sisters and brothers. Retrieved from www.pflag.org/fileadmin/user_upload/An_Open_Letter_12-04.pdf

Flagg, F. (1987). *Fried green tomatoes at the Whistle Stop Café*. New York: Ballantine Books.

Foucault, M. (1982). The subject and power. *Critical Inquiry, 8*(4), 777–795.

Freire, P. (1970). *Pedagogy of the oppressed*. New York: Herder & Herder.

Freire, P. (1987). The importance of the act of reading. In P. Freire & D. Macedo (Eds.), *Literacy: Reading the word and the world* (pp. 29–36). South Hadley, MA: Bergin and Garvey.

Freire, P. (1998). *Pedagogy of freedom: Ethics, democracy, and civic courage*. Lanham, MD: Rowman & Littlefield.

Freire, P., & Macedo, D. (1987). *Literacy: Reading the word and the world*. South Hadley, MA: Bergin and Garvey.

Garofalo, R., Wolf, C., Kessel, S., Palfrey, J., & DuRant, R. H. (1998). The association between health risk behaviors and sexual orientation among a school-based sample of adolescents. *Pediatrics, 101*(5), 895–902.

Giroux, H. A. (1987). Introduction. In P. Freire & D. Macedo, *Literacy: Reading the word and the world* (pp. 1–27). South Hadley, MA: Bergin and Garvey.

Goldblatt, E. C. (1995). *'Round my way: Authority and double-consciousness in three urban high school writers*. Pittsburgh, PA: University of Pittsburgh Press.

Goldman, S. (2008). *Two parties, one tux, and a very short film about* The Grapes of Wrath. New York: Bloomsbury.

Gonzales, J. (2010). Risk and threat in critical inquiry: Vacancies, violations, and vacuums. In M. V. Blackburn, C. T. Clark, L. M. Kenney, & J. M. Smith (Eds.), *Acting out! Combating homophobia through teacher activism* (pp. 74–87). New York: Teachers College Press.

Graves, K. (2009). *And they were wonderful teachers: Florida's purge of gay and lesbian teachers*. Chicago: University of Illinois.

Gray, M. L. (1999). *In your face: Stories from the lives of queer youth*. New York: Harrington Park Press.

Greenbaum, V. (1994). Literature out of the closet: Bringing gay and lesbian texts and subtexts out in high school English. *English Journal, 83*(5), 71–74.

Guber, P. (Producer), Speilberg, S. (Director). (1985). *The color purple* [Film]. Burbank, CA: Warner Brothers.

Gunther, J. (Director). (2005, March 22). *Postcards from Buster: Buster's Sugartime* [TV program]. Columbus, OH: Public Broadcasting Service.

Hall, D. (Producer), Levy, J. (Producer), & Cholodenko, L. (Director). (1999). *High art* [Film]. New York: USA Home Entertainment.

Halverson, E. R. (2007). Listening to the voices of queer youth: The dramaturgical process as identity exploration. In M. V. Blackburn & C. T. Clark (Eds.), *Literacy research for political action and social change* (pp. 153–175). New York: Peter Lang.

Hamilton, G. (1998). Reading Jack. *English Education, 30*(1), 24–43.

Hancock, A. (2007). When multiplication doesn't equal quick addition: Examining intersectionality as a research paradigm. *Perspectives on Politics, 5*(1), 63–79.

Harstock, N. (1990). Foucault on power: A theory for women? In L. J. Nicholson (Ed.), *Feminism/postmodernism* (pp. 157–173). New York: Routledge.

Himmelstein, K. E. W., & Brückner, H. (2010). Criminal-justice and school sanctions against nonheterosexual youth: A national longitudinal study. *Pediatrics, 127*(1), 49–57.

Hoffman, M. (1993). Teaching *Torch Song*: Gay literature in the classroom. *English Journal, 82*(5), 55–58.

Holland, D., Lachicotte Jr., W., Skinner, D., & Cain, C. (1998). *Identity and agency in cultural worlds*. Cambridge, MA: Harvard University Press.

hooks, b. (1994). *Teaching to transgress: Education as the practice of freedom*. New York: Routledge.

hooks, b. (1996). *Reel to real: Race, sex, and class at the movies*. New York: Routledge.

hooks, b. (2000). Homophobia in Black communities. In D. Constantine-Simms (Ed.), *The greatest taboo: Homosexuality in Black communities* (pp. 67–73). Los Angeles: Alyson Books.

Hornberger, N. H. (2000). Afterword. In M. Martin-Jones & K. Jones (Eds.), *Multilingual literacies: Reading and writing different worlds* (pp. 353–367). Philadelphia, PA: Benjamins.

Howe, J. (2005). *Totally Joe*. New York: Ginee Seo Books.

Human Rights Watch. (2001). *American Journal of Health Education, 32*(5), 302–306.

Jackson, J. M. (2007). *Unmasking identities: An exploration of the lives of gay and lesbian teachers*. Lanham, MD: Rowman & Littlefield.

Kenney, L. M. (2010). Being out and reading queer-inclusive texts in a high school English classroom. In M. V. Blackburn, C. T. Clark, L. Kenney, & J. M. Smith (Eds.), *Acting out! Combating homophobia through teacher activism* (pp. 56–73). New York: Teachers College Press.

Kinsey, A. C. (1948). *Sexual behavior in the human male*. Philadelphia, PA: Saunders.

Kinsey, A. C. (1953). *Sexual behavior in the human female*. Philadelphia, PA: Saunders.

Kosciw, J. G. (2004). *The 2003 National School Climate Survey: The school-related experiences of our nation's lesbian, gay, bisexual, and transgender youth*. New York: GLSEN.

Kosciw, J. G., Diaz, E. M., & Greytak, E. A. (2008). *The 2007 National School Climate Survey: The experiences of lesbian, gay, bisexual, and transgender youth in our nation's schools*. New York: GLSEN.

Kumashiro, K. K. (2001). Queer students of color and antiracist, antiheterosexist education: Paradoxes of identity and activism. In K. K. Kumashiro (Ed.), *Troubling intersections of race and sexuality: Queer students of color and anti-oppressive education* (pp. 1–26). Lanham, MD: Rowman & Littlefield.

Lee, A. (Director). (2005). *Brokeback mountain* [Film]. Universal City, CA : Universal Studios Home Entertainment.

Lee, S. (Director). (1986). *She's gotta have it* [Film]. Beverly Hills, CA: MDM DVD.

Levithan, D. (2003). *Boy meets boy*. New York: Knopf.

Lipkin, A. (1995). The case for a gay and lesbian curriculum. In G. Unks (Ed.), *The gay teen: Educational practice and theory for lesbian, gay, and bisexual adolescents* (pp. 31–52). New York: Routledge.

Luberda, J. (2000). *Unassuming positions: Middlemarch, its critics, and positioning theory.* Retrieved from http://www.sp.uconn.edu/~jbl00001/positioning/luberda_positioning.htm

MacGillivray, I. K. (2004). *Sexual orientation and school policy: A practical guide for teachers, administrators, and community activists.* Lanham, MD: Rowman & Littlefield.

MacGillivray, I. K. (2007). *Gay straight alliances: A handbook for students, educators, and parents.* Binghamton, NY: Haworth Press.

Mayo, C. (2001). Civility and its discontents: Sexuality, race, and the lure of beautiful manners. *Philosophy of Education Yearbook*, pp. 78–87.

McCready, L. T. (2004a). Understanding the marginalization of gay and gender non-conforming Black male students. In M. V. Blackburn & R. Donelson (Eds.), Sexual identities and schooling [Special issue]. *Theory into Practice, 43*(2), 136–143.

McCready, L. T. (2004b). Some challenges facing queer youth programs in urban high schools: Racial segregation and denormalizing whiteness. *Journal of Gay and Lesbian Issues in Education, 1*(3), 37–51.

Melvin, A. (2010). Choosing to stay "in" and the significance of race for lesbian teachers in urban classrooms. In M. V. Blackburn, C. T. Clark, L. M. Kenney, & J. M. Smith (Eds.), *Acting out! Combating homophobia through teacher activism* (pp. 127–142). New York: Teachers College Press.

Moje, E. B., & MuQaribu, M. (2003). Literacy and sexual identity. *Journal of Adolescent and Adult Literacy, 47*(3), 204–208.

Mulcahy, R. (2009). *Prayers for Bobby* [TV]. New York: Lifetime Television.

Murray, D. A. B. (2009). *Homophobias.* Durham, NC: Duke University Press.

Murray, K. (1998). An activist forum II: Fault line. In W. Ayers, J. A. Hunt, & T. Quinn (Eds.), *Teaching for social justice* (pp. 131–132). New York: The New Press.

Naylor, G. (1982). *The women of Brewster Place.* New York: Penguin.

Newman, L. (1988). A letter to Harvey Milk. In *A letter to Harvey Milk* (pp. 25–28). Ithaca, NY: Firebrand Books.

Ngo, B. (2003). Citing discourses: Making sense of homophobia and heteronormativity at Dynamic High School. *Equity & Excellence in Education, 36*(2), 115–124.

Pascoe, C. J. (2007). *Dude, you're a fag: Masculinity and sexuality in high school.* Berkeley: University of California Press.

Pratt, M. B. (1984). Identity: Skin, blood, heart. In E. Bulkin, M. B. Pratt, & B. Smith (Eds.), *Yours in struggle: Three feminist perspectives on anti-semitism and racism* (pp. 11–63). Ithaca, NY: Firebrand Books.

Ray, N. (2009). Lesbian, gay, bisexual and transgender youth: An epidemic of homelessness. Retrieved from www.thetaskforce.org/reports_and_research/homeless_youth

Reeves, K. E. (1999). All God's children. *Essence, 30*(7), 220.

Rhoades, M. J., & Wittenberg, D. (2001). *The Phoenix project: 21st century grant application.* Unpublished grant application, Edison Cluster of Philadelphia School District, Philadelphia, PA.

Rich, A. (1980). Compulsory heterosexuality and lesbian existence. *Signs, 5*(4), 631–660.

Rofes, E. (1995). Making our schools safe for sissies. In G. Unks (Ed.), *The gay teenager: Educational practice and theory for lesbian, gay, and bisexual adolescents* (pp. 79–84). New York: Routledge.

Rose, L. (Director). (2000). *The truth about Jane.* [TV]. New York: Lifetime Television.

Sanchez, A. (2007). *The God box.* New York: Simon & Schuster Books for Young Readers.

Schall, J., & Kauffmann, G. (2003). Exploring literature with gay and lesbian characters in the elementary school. *Journal of Children's Literature, 29*(1), 36–45.

Schey, R., & Uppstrom, A. (2010). Activist work as entry-year teachers: What we've learned. In M. V. Blackburn, C. T. Clark, L. Kenney, & J. M. Smith (Eds.), *Acting out! Combating homophobia through teacher activism* (pp. 88–102). New York: Teachers College Press.

Sedaris, D. (1997). *Holidays on ice.* New York: Little Brown.

Smith, J. M. (2010). Overcoming an identity of privilege to support LGBTQ inclusivity in school. In M. V. Blackburn, C. T. Clark, L. Kenney, & J. M. Smith (Eds.), *Acting out!: Combating homophobia through teacher activism* (pp. 114–126). New York: Teachers College Press.

Smith, M. W., & Wilhelm, J. (2002). *"Reading don't fix no Chevys": Literacy in the lives of young men.* Portsmouth, NH: Heinemann.

Spurlin, W. J. (2000). *Lesbian and gay studies and the teaching of English: Positions, pedagogies, and cultural politics.* Urbana, IL: National Council of Teachers of English.

Street, B. V. (1999). The meanings of literacy. In D. A. Wagner, R. L. Venezky, & B. V. Street (Eds.), *Literacy: An international handbook* (pp. 34–40). Boulder, CO: Westview Press.

Streisand, B. (Producer) & Greenwald, M. (Director). (2000). *What makes a family* [TV]. New York: Lifetime Television.

Sumara, D., & Davis, B. (1999). Interrupting heteronormativity: Toward queer curriculum theory. *Curriculum Inquiry, 29*(2), 191–208.

Talburt, S. (2000). *Subject to identity: Knowledge, sexuality, and academic practices in higher education.* Albany: State University of New York Press.

Van Sant, G. (Director). (2008). *Milk* [Film]. Universal City, CA: Universal Studios Home Entertainment.

Vetter, A. M. (2010). "'Cause I'm a G": Identify work of a lesbian teen in language arts. *Journal of Adolescent and Adult Literacy, 54*(2), 98–108.

Vygotsky, L. (1986). *Thought and language.* Cambridge, MA: M.I.T. Press.

Walker, A. (1982). *The color purple.* New York: Harcourt.

Wallace, K. (2005). *Erik & Isabelle: Sophomore year at Foresthill High.* Sacramento, CA: Foglight Press.

Watts, J. (2001). *Finding H. F.* Los Angeles: Alyson Books.

Winterson, J. (1985). *Oranges aren't the only fruit.* New York: Grove/Atlantic Monthly Press.

Index

About the Author

Mollie V. Blackburn is an associate professor of literacy education at The Ohio State University. She co-edited (with Caroline Clark, Lauren Kenney, and Jill Smith) *Acting Out!: Combating Homophobia Through Teacher Activism*. That book was named an "Outstanding Academic Title" by *Choice* magazine and was recognized by the Conference on English Education with the Richard A. Meade Award in English Education. She also co-edited (with Caroline Clark) *Literacy Research for Political Action*. Her scholarship received an award for a body of work from the Queer Studies special interest group of the American Educational Research Association. She is the recipient of the Alan C. Purves Award for articles in *Research in the Teaching of English* that were deemed rich with classroom implications, and the Ralph C. Preston Award for her dissertations that work for social justice.